Losing
the Plot in
Opera

Losing the Plot in Opera

MYTHS AND SECRETS OF THE WORLD'S GREAT OPERAS

BRIAN CASTLES-ONION

metro

Published by Metro Publishing
an imprint of John Blake Publishing Ltd
3 Bramber Court, 2 Bramber Road,
London W14 9PB, England

www.johnblakepublishing.co.uk

First published by Exisle Publishing Limited, New Zealand, 2008
This edition published 2009

ISBN: 978 1 84454 846 0

British Library Cataloguing-in-Publication Data:
A catalogue record for this book is available from
the British Library.

Original text design and production by *BookNZ*
This edition designed by www.envydesign.co.uk

Printed in the UK by CPI William Clowes Beccles NR34 7TL

1 3 5 7 9 10 8 6 4 2

Papers used by John Blake Publishing are natural, recyclable
products made from wood grown in sustainable forests. The
manufacturing processes conform to the environmental regulations
of the country of origin.

For Geraldine and the Babies

CONTENTS

CONTENTS

'Every theatre is an insane asylum, but an opera theatre is the ward for the incurables.'

Franz Schalk, Austrian conductor

ACKNOWLEDGEMENTS

SPECIAL THANKS TO Ian Watt for patiently extracting every word and editing out the rudest bits, and to Benny Thomas for having faith that this book could eventuate in the first place.

To Geraldine Turner for correcting my grammar, putting up with my tantrums when I had writer's block and steadily reminding me that I had another few pages to write ...

To the great Australian baritone, Robert Allman, who supplied a wealth of information (most of which could not go to print!).

To Dame Joan Sutherland and Richard Bonynge and to all my colleagues, past and present, who have not always patiently endured hearing these anecdotes in coffee breaks.

And to the brilliant lyricist Alan Jay Lerner, who once said, 'I have always believed that only genuinely talented people can create something that is genuinely bad. Only the mediocre are always at their best.'

GLOSSARY

Aficionado: Someone to avoid at all times when talking opera.

Aria: A solo moment for the singer, a song.

Bel canto: This translates from the Italian as 'beautiful singing' but is a commonly misused term. Correctly, it refers to a musical and vocal style when drama and perfect singing technique were considered at its peak. These days bel canto means anything from singing fast and high to low and slow. The most eloquent usage comes from the divine Madame Vera Galupe-Borszkh, internationally renowned traumatic soprano, who declares that the vocal life of a soprano has four stages: '1. Bel canto, 2. Can belto, 3. Can't belto, 4. Can't canto'.

Cabaletta: The bit following an aria where the singer suddenly changes his/her mind and sings a more rhythmic tune over a rumpty-tum orchestral accompaniment. If there is a repeat of this cabaletta the singer is advised to embellish the tune with extra notes which appear to the listener to be improvised – but in reality it is well rehearsed. Our heroine, Maria Callas, commented that the first cabaletta was for the composer, the second was for Callas.

Cadence: An harmonic comma or full stop.

Coda: That's all, folks!

Coloratura: The fast runny bits that sometimes thrill an audience.

Comprimario: A performer who specialises in character roles. Although frequently not possessing the most beautiful voice on the stage, this is the person who sometimes supplies the laughs and the irritations.

Continuo: A harpsichord, fortepiano or any museum-type keyboard instrument that plays with the singer during recitatives to keep them in pitch. Continuo players are encouraged to be inventive and embellish their music to enhance the onstage action.

Heldentenor: A dramatic tenor who specialises in the German repertoire. Some opera authorities believe that they are related to the dodo – long extinct.

Interval: A 20-minute pause between acts where you can catch up with friends in the foyer for a drink and chat about anything not related to the performance in hand, or indeed the time to leave a bad performance. Life's too short.

Maestro: God.

Manuscript: The original scribblings of the composer – the holy paper chalice.

Metronome: A mechanical device that produces a regulated beat, measured in beats-per-minute, which enables a performer to play the exact speed that's marked on the sheet music. It's the thing I hated most when I started out learning the piano. It would suddenly go faster or slower than I was playing!

Motif/Leitmotif (tr. 'leading motif' or recurring musical fragment): The little snippet of a recurring tune which composers, especially Richard Wagner, used to remind you of a specific character or dramatic moment in the opera.

Obbligato: An instrumental solo that occurs at the same time as someone is singing. It's like a duet with your favourite instrument.

Podium: The sacred spot in the orchestra pit where the conductor stands. Great performances, not necessarily musical, are regularly seen on this small rise.

Proscenium arch: The archway between the audience and the stage. It's the sometimes elaborate frame that borders the curtain. If you're a performer onstage and not behind the proscenium arch when the curtain comes down, you're going to be very embarrassed.

Recitative: The 'talky' bits between the arias and ensembles. Sometimes there's a tinny harpsichord playing at the same time.

Repertoire: Scheduled operas in an opera

company's season – or the roles an artist would like to sing.

Repetiteur: A musician (often reluctant to be in the public eye) who resembles Rossini's Figaro – a master of all trades. Simply translated, a repetiteur 'repeats' until it's learnt! Not only does he (or she) teach the singers their roles and oversee standards of musicianship and diction, but they also play piano at staging rehearsals, work backstage during performances and assist the conductor. They are also scapegoats for any problems between maestro and artist!

Squillo: The core or edge of the voice that can cut through an orchestra like a sabre.

Stretta: The bit at the end of a musical section that speeds up to boiling point.

Tessitura: The vocal range where the role or aria sits. With most singers, it's always too high.

Testosterone: The manly juice that makes a singer sexy.

Verismo: 'True to life' opera plots that have fairly passionate vocal outbursts with lots of yelling, crying and death.

Vibrato: An expressive and technically modulated vocal tool created by the flow of air as it passes the vocal folds. Used in excess, it can wobble out of control – thus making it hard to distinguish what pitch is intended. In the hands of a sensitive vocal artist, it can resemble the artistry of a fine instrumentalist.

Ensembles

Duet: When one singer is joined by a second singer.

Trio: The stage is getting a little crowded.

Quartet: Far too many egos on stage for one man to handle.

Quintet: Not interested.

Sextet: Let's have fun.

Dynamics

Pianissimo: Very soft – a dynamic never used or understood by an opera singer.

Piano: Soft – or a little softer than you sang the last phrase.

Mezzo piano: Half soft (are you kidding?).

Mezzo forte: Half loud (give me a break!).

Forte: A general volume for a singer.

Fortissimo: Very loud (just in case my fans in the back row can't hear me).

OVERTURE

THIS FUTURE BESTSELLER came about when a publisher from Exisle attended an outdoor opera concert which I conducted and compered, apparently with wit and whimsy. She found the experience at the same time so profound and hysterically funny that she asked me to pen my particular observations about music, singing, opera and the personalities housed therein for the benefit of those who'd like to know more about the opera business. Luckily my memory is such that I recall every little detail from the past – all those anecdotes that singers from previous generations have passed on over the dinner table – as well as the myriad of quirky things that have happened since I started in the industry. I have no idea what I did yesterday but I can tell you, in detail, who sang what, where and what their colleagues thought of them in many performances worldwide over the past fifty years – and who they slept with.

Essentially, I feel a little bit like Marjorie

Kennedy-Fraser when she gathered and preserved the collection of Scottish folksongs that became known as *Songs of the Hebrides*. These little-known treasures of song would have been lost for all eternity had she not spent hours jotting down the tunes and lyrics before they were forgotten. Classical musical whizzes might prefer me to have compared it to those really popular *Chants d'Auvergne* (affectionately known as Ditties of the Aubergine) of Joseph Canteloube but my country upbringing has allowed my musical tastes to be cheerily eclectic.

Goodness only knows how I got myself into this crazy world of opera. It surely wasn't the attraction of a fat lady wearing a metal breastplate, though this can be attractive under the right conditions, but if you need to know how I arrived at this point in my life, here it is in a nutshell.

My parents married just after the Second World War and became the owners of an unwanted second-hand piano that previously belonged to a friend. During the move the delivery men dropped the instrument and it remained unopened and unused in our living room until I, a cute four-year-old, decided I would like to learn to play the instrument properly. Weeks later, I performed my debut recital at a school assembly to display my musical prowess. The repertoire that day was not technically or emotionally taxing (I had considered my audience's youthfulness) so it consisted of selections from the songs from *Mary*

Poppins. From that glamorous moment on, I never looked back.

My early musical passion consisted mainly of Scottish songs. My mother was born in Ayrshire and adored the records of the 'good' Scottish tenor Kenneth McKellar. I also had some weird liking for the records of 1930s film star Jeanette MacDonald. How I got that affliction, I will never know. Fortunately, my parents allowed – nay, encouraged – my musical studies by providing me with several new records every week. That was indeed a big financial outlay on a humble miner's income. Throughout my years at school I was hungry to learn and digest every detail about most aspects of vocal music. With the encouragement of a teacher, I recognised at an early age that the singing voice can communicate better than any instrument especially when united with dramatic text. Therefore I firmly decided to put all my eggs in one basket and forge a career in opera, while keeping my admiration for Kenneth and Jeanette to this day.

I survived high school and university (or should I say that they survived me?) and almost the next day was welcomed onto the music staff of a major opera company. There my life dreams seemed to be complete. Like the naïve Candide of Voltaire (or Bernstein), I was oblivious to the world around me, unaware what vipers and snakes were nearby in the guise of colleagues and management. It was then that I subconsciously decided to remain an ever young Peter Pan figure and observe the craziness that continues to be my professional career. Somehow it paid off. I happily seek out the 'nice folk' with their unique stories, many of which are documented in this book.

Working as a vocal coach is a bit like being a psychologist. A lot of time is spent chatting, listening to the singer vent their anger at whatever is going wrong in their life and enduring the depressions when the voice is not responding as desired. Love-life and career are almost inseparable. Since the voice is the mirror to the soul, the singer has to feel secure with the coach because every aspect of his or her personality is on display in its rawest form. The slightest musical or vocal correction can trigger a tirade of emotion from the singer. Then the coach has to expel unlimited volumes of energy to stabilise the stricken singer before the next patient is due. At the end of the day, the coach feels emotionally and psychologically exhausted! Did I make the move to the conductor's podium to free myself of that daily draining of energy? Perhaps.

Almost everyone connected with the opera business is peculiar. Their idiosyncratic behaviour is encouraged – after all, they're artists. If you think gossip magazines are trashy, well this book far exceeds that quota. Of course, it's not all about opera. Life inside the opera house is much like what some of us experience at home, from well-known tantrums by principal artists to the conductor who meditates upside down and naked in his dressing room before a performance.

During intervals I usually chat to each of the principal singers and encourage them to maintain their good performance for the next act. Once that bit of ego pampering is over, you'll usually find me gossiping with the make-up artists in the wig room. Like friendly hairdressers, they have the low-down on everyone. Their duties finish long after the stage performance has ended. They have to prepare the wig in readiness for the next performance as well as clean off the glue residue which sticks the hairpiece to the singer's head.

Financial supporters play a major part in the production of opera. They have always been a necessary part of the industry but, in the present climate, we really cannot do without them. Part of my job is to attend functions, cocktail parties, dinners to help make these supporters feel a part of the company. One soprano of a few generations past told me that singing is a little like prostitution: you're paid by the client to perform on cue. This is sad but true. The patron's understanding of the lowly paid singer is sometimes beyond their comprehension and most of the time an artist's income in no way compares to that of a patron. A few years ago a woman of enormous wealth engaged me in conversation and we discovered that we were both fond of dogs. Her poodle, Clarence, was one of the joys of her life, but she had to find a suitable dog-sitter for him when she was out of the country. On a recent trip overseas, this wealthy opera and dog-lover was in Cartier's in Paris and decided to purchase a diamond-studded collar for Clarence. Not knowing the exact size to buy (diamonds can be expensive) she called home – several thousand miles away and in a different time zone – and asked the dog-sitter, who was on trial, to measure Clarence's neck and provide her with a sizing. 'Do you realise what time it is here? It's seven o'clock in the morning. I'm not going to wake him!' the nanny exclaimed. Instead of being angry, our patron was overjoyed. She knew she had found the right dog-sitter!

Without further ado, let's get going. You must remember that all tales contained within are true. They have been lovingly selected, collated and reported just as they were passed on to me by my colleagues. Some may seem extreme, but that's opera. Grab a coffee and a plate of chocolate biscuits, just as we do in the green room, and eavesdrop at the dressing room door of a little boy from the country who became an opera conductor.

THE
CONDUCTOR

THE CONDUCTOR IS the boss of the opera production. What he/she says goes. I have witnessed intricate staging, painstakingly rehearsed by directors and cast for weeks, being overturned, or shot down in flames, by conductors at the final stage rehearsals. 'Just stand at the front of the stage, look at me and sing,' the conductor screams at the singers as the director sulks in a corner. 'You want to please me, don't you?' the conductor adds with a satisfied smile.

And yet a lot of people think that conducting is easy. How hard can it be to stand there and wave your arms about? The orchestra knows how it goes, doesn't it? The guy in the penguin suit must surely be there for show.

As the American composer Stephen Sondheim once wrote, 'Art isn't easy.' There's a lot more to it than that. Apart from having to know the score intimately and being able to cue each instrument and singer at the important times, the conductor's reading or interpretation is what the audience experiences. Well, in an ideal world that's the way it should be. The conductor is responsible for applying the correct musical and theatrical style to the work at hand while allowing the composer's intention to shine. In most cases this does not occur.

It might be news to you that orchestral conductors sneer at opera conductors. There's an unmentioned ranking system in every aspect of the arts. Opera singers look down on music theatre performers. Operetta is looked upon as 'lighter' fare and easier to sing than opera, which is certainly not true. Orchestral conductors who have never ventured into the realm of opera don't realise what a challenge it is to marry music and words. Each enhances the other. It's pure theatrical magic. If only the orchestral conductors understood that the great works of the operatic repertoire can be just as orchestrally interesting as a Mahler symphony or a Beethoven concerto.

Many of the great operatic composers have been profound orchestrators, supplying the theatrical colour that complements and assists the onstage action. Pit players rarely reach fulfilment in performance because the person on the podium fails to include them in that action. When orchestral players are led by a great artist the result is poetry in motion.

Opera conductors fit into three particular categories, the Maestro, the Routiner and the

Hack. Let's get the latter two over and done with *prestissimo*. When an orchestral player asks another, 'Who's carving tonight?' it means that the orchestra has been led by a conductor of the Hack variety for too long. There is a myriad of conductors who mount the podium and simply beat time. Sometimes, by chance, it happens to be a suitably correct tempo but little thought or honest emotion is delivered. Smiling at the band to suggest 'Aren't we having a lovely time?' isn't good enough either. Routiners, on the other hand, are competent but display nothing of their own personality. They are conductors of experience, authority and a certain prestige who perform with competence but without individual flair. They are hardly inspiring but many conductors are content to be enrolled in this school of dullsville – or are simply unaware of their mediocrity. After all, mediocre performers are at their best all the time!

A Maestro gives life to the score, takes command and makes everyone feel secure under his baton. Some have very big batons, others small and a special few have none at all. We must remember that it's how they use them that counts. The orchestra is swept up with the power of the reading and the onstage singers feel so comfortable that they deliver their very best performance. How many times have you seen that happen in an opera house?

When opera began several hundred years ago it was the singer who was the star. In the middle of the last century the conductor took the lead and now, it seems, the productions are more important than the music. These days an audience doesn't really care who's singing as long as the singer looks okay and the production appears to be expensive. Every now and then a celebrity is the focus of the performance but, in the current climate, a 'celebrity' is someone who has won a competition or your next-door neighbour who has appeared on a television reality programme.

Conductors can be crazy creatures. Many believe that the world revolves totally around them which, in many opera companies, it does. I've seen stage managers destroyed by temperamental conductors. An assistant chorus master missing a cue in an early stage rehearsal was dragged onstage – in front of the cast, orchestra and crew – and humiliated and sacked by the conductor. I've seen singers demoralised just before they go onstage, but rarely is the conductor confronted in such a way. Some maestri strut into the rehearsal room on the first day of production and expect their opinions and needs to be observed by everyone. The 'eyebrows down' expression favoured by some initially scares but the upbeat reveals everything there is to know. If the conductor doesn't know the score, or what he or she is doing, it's evident to all. Some can fake a great deal by emoting with the flow of the music: some have had long and successful careers doing this. I relish the memory of a noted conductor, during an ensemble call of a Monteverdi opera, trying to persuade a mezzo soprano to come with him on a musical point – 'You trust me. Don't you?' Her reply was a straight and honest 'No'. She was right but her candour didn't win her any Brownie points. The rest of the cast congratulated her afterwards – a long time afterwards.

Other conductors can be delightfully crazy. A young conductor knocked on an old Italian maestro's dressing room door and entered to find the lovable musician working in the toilet. He was painting white-out liquid onto used satay sticks, dripping the fluid all over the cistern and bowl. 'Isn't this great? I make batons for free!' The young conductor nodded in agreement then made a hasty, if confused, exit. The same aged maestro would denounce orchestral players if he felt they didn't agree with his approach. He did this with regularity until one French horn player revolted: 'And I denounce you back'. Following a complaint that he continually used broken batons (or white satay sticks) for his performances, the maestro conducted Verdi's *Falstaff*, a rather delicate and tricky score, with a twig he'd found on the way to the theatre.

Opera conductors of the old school could and would comment on the stage performance during a show with a paying audience behind them. Some have been known to hold their noses and pull an imaginary toilet chain if the onstage vocal performance displeased them. They might even take off their shoe and sniff it to display a more sensitive criticism. It has been known for the maestro to call out 'why you sing so horrible?' in a voice reminiscent of the Godfather. It's true. I was there.

I was playing a rehearsal of Puccini's one-act opera *Il Tabarro* (The Cloak), a wonderful work. The story plays out on a barge in Paris. Michele, the baritone, and his wife Giorgetta, the soprano (because Puccini didn't write any good roles for mezzos), are in a loveless marriage. Because Giorgetta is bored, she is having an affair, perhaps only in her mind, with Luigi, the tenor who is attempting to portray a stevedore, and they plan to run off that night. Before this can happen Michele strangles him and covers the body with his cloak. He calls Giorgetta, who has been waiting endlessly for her Luigi, and uncovers his dead body. Hence the title of the opera.

Anyway, Giorgetta is a very sexy creature. Her music suggests great passion as well as sexual frustration. The soprano playing her in this particular production was far from fulfilling the dramatic requirements of the role. Just at the most inappropriate time, at the end of the week when we were all tired and emotionally on edge, the sensitive Italian maestro pronounced in the same Godfather voice, 'You sing like potato'. The soprano stopped. 'Sorry Maestro, what did you say?' 'You sing like potato', he repeated, then added, 'You have all the sex of a potato!' Oddly enough she ran out of the room in tears and we all had an early break. Actually, the maestro was exactly right. Giorgetta's husband calls her 'scalandrina' meaning 'slut'. You can't be a slut if you're a potato.

There are the Slavic maestri who look at you and say, 'Come on, we make' as they do the downbeat so quickly that they reduce the opera's playing time by fifteen minutes. That type of conductor would be a great taxi driver. One such colleague, if you can call a conductor a colleague, mistakenly conducted six in a bar instead of four in a section of Act Two of Verdi's *Otello*. When I pointed out this minute mistake, he insisted that this was how he always did it. For the remainder of the production he kept it in six – to the surprise of the orchestra, who followed the six but played four. At his best, he gave vividly vibrant performances that lifted the audience out of their seat. At his worst, he was just plain vulgar.

We have happy memories of moments when an internationally renowned Mozart specialist, with the full orchestra in front of him, began the exceedingly well-known penultimate scene in *Don Giovanni*. The scenery on stage falls, as directed, in time to the crashing chords that herald the appearance of the stone guest who comes to drag Don Giovanni down to hell (or the green room cafeteria). The full weight of the orchestra is heard and the respected conductor cues the bass portraying the commendatore's statue for the famous 'Don Giovanni', which should make the walls of the theatre shake. At this moment in the rehearsal nothing happened. There was absolute silence. An even larger cue was given almost dislocating the pompous conductor's arm. Again the bass didn't sing. The conductor asked in a frustrated voice, 'Why don't you sing when I give you the cue?' The bass responded wryly, 'You cued me two bars early!' And he was correct. Moments like these prove that there is a God. The question used to be: If you saw a conductor and a viola player walking down the street and you had to kill them both, which one would you kill first? Answer: The conductor. Business before pleasure.

Some older conductors like to unbalance or confuse younger colleagues by offering unsolicited strange advice. Going into the pit one night a friend was stopped at the pit entrance by a conductor who had led the production in a previous season. He offered the following deliberately subversive advice: 'All you have to do is work out if it starts up or down'. This puzzling piece of information stuck with the young man throughout the performance. Fortunately he managed to work out which direction the upbeat was and went on to carve out a decent career on the podium. The older gentleman, no longer his mentor, retired soon afterwards.

Sadly, characters like the old Italian maestro, or even the Slavic conductor are no longer appearing on the world's stages. Personalities seldom mount the podium. They have been replaced by academics and human metronomes. But when a great maestro mounts the podium you will know it. The audience is transported from curtain rise to the magnificent opera bows. (Aren't the bows wonderful too? The best acting of the night.)

LA BOHÉME

Dear Rodolfo,
Son, you've got a charming studio and lovely
roommates, but did you have to get a fourth-
floor walk-up? Do you want to see me in an
early grave? I know it's an L-shaped studio
with an alcove, but four people! I'm not going
to ask who sleeps where. If you had a normal
job like your brother, Stanley, you'd be living
in a nice one-bedroom in an elevator building.
And believe me, your neighbours are a bunch
of characters. That girl on five is a real floozy
and a lousy seamstress. I don't know, other
beatniks are very happy in Greenwich Village;
mine had to schlep off to France.
Your Mother

IT'S AMAZING THAT a music theatre work written
in 1896 is still a hit with audiences. If you ask a
group of opera aficionados to name their handful
of favourites it's most likely that Giacomo Puccini's

La Bohème will feature heavily in their choices. Why? Perhaps it has something to do with the passion of the musical score, the simple poignancy of the plot, the fact that no matter what indulgence a director, conductor or singer might bring to this particular work, it will come up trumps. Perhaps the greatest blooper in operatic criticism was printed in the *New York Times* about the premiere performance of *La Bohème*: 'I cannot believe that there is permanent success for an opera constructed as this one is'. It doesn't get the prize for grammar either.

Over the years, *La Bohème* has been subject to artistic destruction from tatty 'traditional' productions to racy modern updates – even a 2003 season on Broadway where it appeared alongside productions of modern musical shows. As 'operas are just old musicals', this doesn't really create a problem for me. In fact it was a personal delight to note the high percentage of young people in attendance, presumably an audience that had never been to a traditional opera house.

Puccini wrote specifically for his audience. He had a precise perspective on matters of theatre – the concentration span of an audience, the need for drama and the need to maintain melody in opera. In the mid-1890s, he was creating melodious scores when other composers were freeing themselves of tunes. He wrote arias, duets and ensembles and his scores were riddled with melodies that both 'speak' to the audience and enhance the onstage drama.

The world of Italian opera was thrown on its ears in 1890 when Pietro Mascagni wrote his one-act work *Cavalleria Rusticana*. It dealt with a young, ex-army officer who has a pregnant ex-girlfriend and has just left his already married girlfriend. This was not the sort of story that opera-goers were used to seeing on their stages. This 'true to life' soap opera genre was called verismo and influenced a new generation of, especially, Italian composers. Except for the roles in his final opera, *Turandot*, Puccini's characters usually drew on the innocent, next-door-neighbour variety of person. Let's have a closer look at these ingredients as used in *La Bohème*.

When the curtain goes up, we find ourselves in a garret in Paris. We're quickly introduced to the baritone Marcello, a painter, and the tenor, Rodolfo, a poet, both struggling students with a zest for life. Puccini crafts a wave of musical energy for their whimsical banter as they complain about the cold. Naturally, they use the manuscript of Rodolfo's drama to fuel the fire. Two friends, the philosopher Colline (a bass) and the musician Schaunard (a baritone) enter, bringing with them food, wood, wine and money. So onstage we have a tenor, two baritones and a bass pretending they're students. Gone are the days when the Rodolfo was short and rotund. An audience today expects to believe what they see onstage, so younger singers with movie-star looks are now frequently engaged to perform these roles. Some of them can actually sing too.

Next follows a rather nice scene where they are visited by the landlord Benoit. Musically it's a very tricky scene with interjections by all onstage as they get out of paying the month's rent. In my first and only audition for an opera company for the position of repetiteur, the requested repertoire was the Act One finale of Mozart's *Così fan Tutte*, the Act Two finale of *The Marriage of Figaro*, the composer's aria from *Ariadne auf Naxos* (this opera by Richard Strauss was quite unknown to me at the time and I managed to prepare the wrong excerpt) and an ensemble of my own choice. Rather than offer the standard *Carmen* quintet or *Rigoletto* quartet, an old baritone suggested that the audition panel would be impressed if I sang and played the Benoit scene from *La Bohème*. I need not add that they were impressed and that I was immediately offered my first 'professional' job.

Benoit is a cameo role usually cast as an aged, well-known baritone or bass. He need not have too much left in the vocal department but should be brimming with charm. In some productions, this same artist will be engaged to perform the role of Alcindoro in Act Two but we'll get to that after we've met some more of the players.

With the landlord gone, the guys decide that the timing is perfect to get on with Act Two and leave for the Café Momus as it's Christmas Eve. It's all right for them but we still have to meet the soprano love interest and the tenor and soprano have to sing an aria each as well as a duet. Colline, Marcello and Schaunard leave the garret and Rodolfo sits down to catch up on some work before joining them in the next act. As he puts pen to paper, beautifully described by a trilling tune of a flute in the orchestra, there's a knock at the door.

Rodolfo: Chi e la? (Who's there?)

Mimi (Still behind the door): Scusi.

Rodolfo: A woman!

Mimi: My candle's gone out.

If you thought that this was the fastest pick-up line in opera wait to see what happens next …

Mimi (real name Lucia) enters the room and immediately faints. (Because some sopranos aren't too clever in the acting department, this moment can sometimes look a little contrived.) Rodolfo admires her attractive looks while she's out to it on the sofa. Reviving, she again requests a light for her candle but it's blown out by the wind. Magically and with a hint of theatricality, Rodolfo's candle is extinguished as Mimi manages to drop the key to her apartment. (Did I tell you that Mimi lives in a neighbouring room? Probably, she's planned the whole scenario.) As they fumble around on the floor searching for the key, their hands meet and they realise it's high time to get better introduced.

Holding her frozen fingers, Rodolfo tells Mimi about himself. 'Sono un poeta' (I'm a poet). 'I have no money but am a millionaire in spirit.' His aria –

more generally known by its first line 'Che gelida manina' (How cold your hand) – ends with Rodolfo asking Mimi to tell her story too. As she does, you realise that she's a fragile woman who's not long for this world. In fact, Puccini cryptically writes fate motifs into her aria. Every time she sings about the coming of spring, the orchestral harmonies and colour change to a minor key. This is Puccini letting us know that she's not going to make it that far.

There are more things that Mimi relates in this aria, 'Mi chiamano Mimi' (They call me Mimi). She describes her work and explains that flowers she embroiders for a living take her far away from her small room and out into the great wide world. She forgets to inform Rodolfo that she is in the early stages of consumption but we find that out soon enough.

Both arias are beautifully crafted, musically and dramatically. Like the greatest of storytellers, Rodolfo takes Mimi on the journey of his life to this moment and lets her in on his aspirations. As his poetic side becomes more fervent, so does Puccini's music. His voice rises to a high C as he sings 'la speranza' (hope). This musical phrase will be quoted at appropriate times throughout the rest of the score. Mimi's aria has less bravado than her tenor colleague's but she has every opportunity to shine. Remember that the dying girl always gets the sympathy vote. With the male cast members calling to Rodolfo from the street below (actually in the wings with a music staff conductor keeping them in rhythm), tenor and soprano rapidly decide that they're made for each other and sing a love duet that closes the act.

These twelve minutes or so of music – two arias and a duet – are familiar items in concert programmes, where the offstage voices of Marcello, Schaunard and Colline are omitted. Unfortunately, the score requires tenor and soprano to leave the stage while singing their final phrase which, incidentally, includes a high C from the soprano and, more often than not, the tenor. The orchestra diminishes in volume so the offstage voices can be lightly audible. When you're on the concert platform, it's hard to make this sound right.

When coaching a singer, it is sometimes rewarding to win an argument on vocal matters rather than be shot down and made to look like a fool. It is generally accepted that, as the pitch of a note goes higher, the sung vowel becomes more open. So, you will generally hear a top C only sung as an 'Ah'. Less technically confident singers will change to that same 'Ah' vowel at a much lower pitch. Tenors sometimes go to the extreme with it. I have heard a wonderfully charismatic soprano say to the conductor, who has asked why she doesn't sing the 'Eh' or 'Ih' to make sense of the word, 'Honey, that's a G. You get an "Ah".' Sure enough, we did – but the sound on that G was absolutely glorious. When dealing with tenors you're also dealing with the most fragile of egos. Ask them to modify a vowel on a highish note and you dice with certain death. Lots of tenors love singing Rodolfo, and most would probably sing the role every night of their career. It's a perfect fit for their voice. Rodolfo's final outburst is the loudest possible 'Mimi!' on that famous G sharp. If that wasn't hard enough, Puccini makes him repeat the same phrase on the same pitch. Sure enough, any tenor will muster the skill, the technique and the force to pronounce her name correctly. Could you imagine hearing him cry 'Mama! Mama!' over the dead body?

Act Two is ablaze with colour and noise. It opens with street sellers calling their wares, street urchins and children (one very spoilt) viewing the festivities. Added to this chaos we have Mimi, Rodolfo and friends enjoying the conversation at Café Momus. Even though Act Two plays only 16 minutes, Puccini has packed the score with some of his most wonderfully honest and intimate music. Listen especially for Rodolfo's short lyrical outburst as Mimi shops for a bonnet. It is a moment filled with the joys of youth, like Stephen Sondheim's 'Being Alive' only much shorter, in the verismo style and in Italian.

High cackling interrupts the moment and Marcello's ex Musetta arrives playing with her dog Lulu and escorted by a wealthy admirer, Alcindoro. As mentioned earlier, you could be seeing the same guy who performed Benoit in Act

One but in different make-up and costume. Marcello ignores her coquettish behaviour so she sings a waltz song, 'Quando me'n vo' soletta per la via (As I wander merrily through the streets), to gain his attention. (Did you ever hear Della Reece's fabulous 'pop' version of this aria titled 'Don't You Know?') In the course of the opera, the action goes straight on without room for audience applause. Musetta pretends to have hurt her ankle and everyone joins in singing an ensemble version of her waltz. As before, the music doesn't stop after the climactic end of the ensemble but I've never experienced a performance when there isn't huge applause at this point – even with bad singers. Such is the power of the score.

Musetta is back in Marcello's favour. Alcindoro has gone offstage looking for a shoe for her. Schaunard realises that he is unable to pay the bill so he and friends depart. A street band is heard offstage and, as it gets nearer, and louder, Alcindoro returns as the waiter hands him the bill. I'm sure that in 1896 the audience found all this very funny.

Usually, performances of *La Bohème* run the first two acts together with a short pause as the Café Momus set is put in place. More adventurous and expensive productions use hydraulics to move between the intimacy of the garret and the Parisian street. One recent production in which I was involved was updated to the 1980s and featured an entire apartment building where one could see

Mimi feasting on a rice dish in her room. The audience could see another, totally unrelated, apartment where an aged couple watched television throughout the whole act. That was quite distracting as the audience wondered who they could be. Directors should understand that 'focus' is of utmost importance. Worse, as Rodolfo and Mimi began the duet that closes the act, the set moved up (not too smoothly or quietly) to expose the next set, a Chinese restaurant that became Café Momus. Musetta sang her aria into a substitute microphone that was actually a tomato sauce bottle. What this had to do with the flavour of Puccini's score bewildered me, as did the fact that, in the 1980s, Mimi would have had suitable medication to clear up her consumption. Why didn't they think of that?

Another Italian composer, Ruggiero Leoncavallo, had a massive success in 1892 with his *Pagliacci*, an hour-long opera concerning a touring theatre company that goes terribly wrong one night. He longed for a second stab at fame with his own *La Bohème*, which premiered in 1897. Apparently Leoncavallo was in the audience on Puccini's opening night in 1896. Can you imagine how depressed he must have been after hearing that brilliant combination of music and drama? Still, Leoncavallo completed his version and it has had moderate success on the operatic stage.

Act Three is perhaps the most concise of all of Puccini's work – and that's saying something.

Following an abrupt start to take you immediately to the stage action, we are shown the daily routine of street sweepers and guardsmen at a toll house at a gate to the city of Paris. From inside a tavern we can hear the ladies' chorus singing in close harmony and then the voice of Musetta is heard quoting two phrases of her waltz song. Obviously this is the only tune she knows. She was lucky that Puccini gave the 'seconda donna' anything at all to sing, let alone a hit song.

We hear the rising phrase of Mimi's tune along with a violent cough from the girl herself. She enters and asks to speak with Marcello. This is the first of five sections that make up the musical drama of this act. In an impassioned outburst Mimi confesses that Rodolfo has abandoned her (this is a nice way of letting us know that they've been living together) but she is unaware that he's currently sleeping in a nearby tavern. As her pleading with Marcello dies down, Rodolfo appears at the door as Mimi runs and conceals herself behind part of the set. She listens intently as Rodolfo tells the reason for their split. Initially, it's just the usual stuff that divorces are made of but he finally lets on that he fears her health is quickly fading. This particular section – a trio – is one of the most moving few pages in the entire operatic repertoire. As Rodolfo sings his wavelike melody, Mimi interjects with gasps of horror as she realises she's going to die before the final curtain. The orchestra swells in volume as Mimi sobs her heart out. If you don't shed a tear at this point of the show, you're made of rock. Mimi's uncontrollable sobbing is loud enough for even the onstage tenor to notice and they run into each other's arms.

This is the perfect opportunity for another aria from Mimi, and she doesn't let us down. In the most poignant way she farewells Rodolfo with the message that she's going back to where she was before they met. She'll collect her few worldly possessions but asks him to keep the little pink bonnet as a souvenir of their love: 'Addio, senza rancore' (Goodbye, and no hard feelings). If only all relationships ended so calmly … This leads straight into a quartet – actually a duet with Marcello and Musetta bickering at each other behind Mimi and Rodolfo – which concludes the act. Our principal tenor and soprano say farewell to their time together, their voices riding on a charming tune that was originally composed as the song 'Sole e amore' (Sun and love), which Puccini wrote for the magazine *Paganini* in 1888. The song ends with a rather cute dedication written in the vocal line: 'Al *Paganini*, G. Puccini'. For some unknown reason, an internationally renowned soprano always includes this number in her recitals and invites the accompanist to join her in duet on the final page. Yes, I have vocalised with the best. Puccini even used the original piano accompaniment as the basis for his orchestration when he reworked the number as the closing minutes of Act Three. To tie the whole thing together, he finished the same way he started – with an abrupt, jolting chord.

Act Four finds us back in the garret with Rodolfo and Marcello bemoaning the loss of their respective girlfriends. They sing what is really the only new tune left in the opera, two soliloquies that blend as a duet, 'Ah Mimi, tu più non torni' (Ah, Mimi, will you not return?) Puccini, a master of theatre, knows that audiences don't need new ideas in the closing pages of a tragic romance. It's good to remind them of what has happened previously – and music quickly establishes itself in the memory and Puccini lays it on thick. Thereafter, almost everything that you hear is a reworking of a tune, a motif or phrase that happened in Act One.

Schaunard and Colline arrive (remember them?) and rapidly get into some comic dancing as Musetta enters to stop the party. Her news is terrible. Mimi's illness has worsened and she wants to die in Rodolfo's arms. Mimi staggers in and is made comfortable on a bed. In the early days of *La Bohème* performances it is said that the great Italian tenor, Enrico Caruso, a regular prankster, would have a chamber pot placed under the bed to be revealed when the bed was moved for Mimi's entrance. Legend has it that he also pressed a warm sausage into her tiny frozen hand to warm it in Act One. Those were the days.

Musetta and Marcello depart to sell Musetta's earrings to get money for medicine while Colline and Schaunard leave to pawn Colline's coat. He sings a sentimental ballad to his faithful coat 'Vecchia zimarra' (Old coat). In one 'modern' production, he sang this while sitting on the toilet. I don't think so.

The world's greatest tenor was again the subject of a rather intriguing story. For one matinée performance in January 1916, Caruso, Frances Alda, Antonio Scotti and Andres de Segurola were in the cast of *La Bohème* in Philadelphia. Segurola, who was playing Colline, turned to the Rodolfo (Caruso) and whispered hoarsely, 'I've lost my voice.' Caruso responded with, 'Non fa niènte. You just stand still and move your lips and I'll sing it for you.' With his back to the audience he sang the bass aria. Legend has it that the audience was quite unaware of the problem on stage or that they were witnessing an historic moment. Enrico Caruso later recorded the aria as a party record. The flip side of the disc featured reminiscences from New Zealand-born soprano Alda about the event.

Left alone, Mimi and Rodolfo recall their past happiness supported by several of the wonderful tunes from Act One. Mimi askes for 'la mia cuffietta' (My muff) to warm her hands. In one performance of the famous Baz Luhrmann production with set and customes updated to 1957 Paris, Rodolfo couldn't locate her 'cuffietta' so he presented her with a car wheel hubcap. Mimi gave a little smile that wasn't in the original show's direction.

The others return, and while Musetta prays

aloud, Mimi dies. Schaunard gets to inform everyone on stage that Mimi's dead – although Puccini had already given us a fairly good idea from the theatrical 'death' chord. Rodolfo cries out Mimi's name and sobs hysterically as the curtain falls.

TRISTAN UND ISOLDE

IN 1867, GOOD old Gioacchino Rossini said, 'Wagner has lovely moments but awful quarters of an hour.' Mark Twain wrote in his 1924 autobiography, 'I have been told that Wagner's music is better than it sounds.' Let's stand to agree on the former?

The trouble with the operas of Richard Wagner is that you either love them or hate them. There is no halfway measure in the appreciation of this unique repertoire. Audience responses to his operas are usually rapturous. I can't confirm if that is because they are so moved by the emotion of the drama and music or if they need to move their hands to get the body's circulation moving.

Don't for an instant think that I disapprove of the German maestro's oeuvre. In my early childhood, the voice of the Norwegian soprano Kirsten Flagstad introduced me to the profundities of Brünnhilde's immolation. That impressive, and still awesome, recording from 1935 remains a benchmark against which all my other Brünnhildes are measured. That particular musical chunk is, perhaps, the most accessible and typical of Wagner's operatic scenes. It comes at the conclusion of the famous Ring Cycle – a quartet of operas that make a 20-hour journey through the story of the Ring of the Nibelungs. The immolation scene, from *Götterdämmerung*, itself lasts about 20 minutes. In it, Brünnhilde, a loud-voiced warrior princess, rides her horse into the flames holding a golden ring. We needn't get into the story because it's a different opera, but the emotion, the orgasmic surge of the orchestra and the drama onstage are an ample reward for enduring the whole show. Luckily my initial immolation experience hooked me and inspired me to explore what else Wagner had written.

Why does the name of Wagner conjure up images of fat ladies in horned helmets and metal breastplates? For some rather mean reason, history has not treated Wagner favourably. Even if you look at original cast photographs, the performers are not portly. They typify the look of the day – solemn and serious – and the same images and poses can be seen in other opera shots. Unfortunately, Wagner held some sort of hold on the design concept of his productions worldwide, similar to the *Phantom of the Opera*, *Cats* or *Les Misérables* today. Audiences had to wait for over half a century for even mild updating of a Wagner work, and now we can expect to see almost anything when the curtain rises. Two of the composer's works don't really merit 'extreme' productions. *Die Meistersinger von Nürnberg* and *Tristan und Isolde* are what they are and even the most outrageous director would not tamper with either setting or time when presenting a 'new' production. Medieval Nurnberg can really only have one look and you really require something that looks like a ship for your Tristan story. But imaginative designers and directors have placed their own stamp on their productions.

I feel fortunate that my only *Tristan* experience was with a director and designer who trusted Wagner's monumental score. Their set beautifully reflected the transparency of the orchestral colours and allowed the focus to be entirely on the performers. Our cast was articulate, warm voiced and beautiful of appearance. The audience experienced something that would, I believe, have also pleased Wagner. It was a complete music theatre experience and one was unaware of its more than four-hour duration. (I've always insisted that nothing in theatre should be longer than three hours but I allowed this one exception.) Let me describe the single set. The floor of the stage was a pool of water. Hanging above that sea of water was a perspex raked stage supported by ropes suggesting a ship. That was all the audience needed to fire the flames of fantasy for the rest of the performance.

Singers who specialise in performing Wagner

roles are particular. Offstage you might find them the antithesis of their onstage character (unless we're talking about basses, who never change their mood no matter which side of the footlights they are(. In rehearsal and in the green room, a Wagner soprano will have the loudest laugh, she'll want to know all the gossip and listen to every crude joke. She will even offer some crudity of her own. It's easy to hear that her cackling laughter sounds exactly like Brünnhilde's battle cry 'Ho yo to ho', so clearly is her voice placed in the singing resonance. It's as if she's always vocalising. Wagner sopranos cultivate a needle-like core to the voice that will cut through any orchestra like a laser beam. That's a necessity because her voice must 'ride' the orchestral waves at those big moments. If her voice gets covered and lost, the point of her vocal message vanishes. Conductors, take heed. At these points in the music, the soprano prepares in advance, musters the vocal cut and sails to victory. This is the essence of a Wagnerian diva.

The very greatest have an added vocal warmth that keeps the sound 'feminine'. Contemporary accounts affirm that the great Kirsten Flagstad's voice warmly enveloped each and every member in the audience. So, too, her replacement at New York's Metropolitan Opera, Helen Traubel, delivered a luscious warm sound while able to conjure up the required belt or volume. She was born and bred in America, where she performed in night clubs and in Hollywood films. I don't know whether this story is true or not, but one of her colleagues alleged that Traubel was lazy. Her daily sessions with her rehearsal pianist – sessions that were meant to maintain the vocal and physical stamina for the long and demanding Wagner roles – became less frequent and were regularly cancelled. The pianist had the gift of being able, at sight, to transpose the printed score up and down in pitch. If Traubel was feeling less energetic, she would ask that the role be rehearsed down. It got to be that every rehearsal was at that lower pitch. Eventually, she found that she could only sing it at that pitch – and her opera career came to a rapid halt. Traubel had charisma and charm. In her vocal heyday her Isolde was a thing of great beauty.

In modern times, Isolde has been 'owned' (if anyone can own a role) by the Swedish soprano Birgit Nilsson. For many, she was seen as the successor to Flagstad though she was a very different kind of singer. Although her laser-like sound was also linked to Puccini's *Turandot* (she was partly responsible for reviving interest in the opera) and other Puccini and Verdi roles, she was primarily a Wagner singer. Her sound, her demeanour, even her profile, suited the Wagner productions of the 1960s and 1970s. When asked in interview what it took to sing the role of Isolde, Nilsson responded, 'A comfortable pair of shoes!' (Actually, this was originally said by Flagstad, but we won't let that get in the way of a good story.)

The greatest Tristan in living memory was the

Danish tenor Lauritz Melchior, the helden tenor equal of Flagstad and Traubel. His voice, though not particularly lovely, had all the heft, squillo (or vocal ping) and energy to maintain this long, arduous role. Tristan obviously suited him and he made the role sound natural. If there were any Wagner performer of that period who was chubby, it was Melchior. His colleagues had waistlines, but Melchior was a lovable tubby who appeared like your favourite uncle. In fact, he had quite a career in films in the 1950s, usually playing uncles or grandfathers who had been opera singers. Producers inserted scenes where he would sit at the piano (in a cabin onboard a luxury liner) and sing excerpts from Wagner operas. In what type of film would you see that happen today? Lauritz Melchior lived in a ritzy apartment in New York and would use the swimming pool in the hotel as his bathtub. Legend has it that it was Melchior who, when missing his cue to enter on the swan in *Lohengrin*, asked, 'What time does the next swan leave?'

Tristan und Isolde, a work in three acts, is held by many critics to be the greatest setting of a love story for the opera stage. The opening prelude (or vorspiel) immediately puts you in the mood for the rest of the show. It begins with what we call the 'Tristan' motif. Motifs are tunes, or fragments of tunes, that represent a particular character or emotion. Wagner's musical language is based on them and he uses them masterfully, enhancing the dramatic situation by quoting another idea. With few exceptions, these motifs can be just a handful of notes. It's the intervals and rhythm that form them that make them instantly recognisable. For instance, Tristan has a motif consisting of seven notes starting with a moderate interval jump, followed by a winding chromatic climb. Every time Wagner wants you to think of Tristan, or if another character is singing about him, you hear this motif in the orchestra. Of course, Isolde has her motif too. Hers only lasts four notes but those important rising intervals leave you hanging suspended. Wagner also provides a 'Tristan chord' on the menu. By the time the first act is over, we've been introduced to nearly 20 of these motifs and our musical tummies are quite full. You don't need to know about them before you go to the opera; nor are they overstated by the composer. They're heard in tasteful abundance whenever necessary.

Wagner's orchestral music often darts around finding pauses only on unresolved chords. The instrumental solos wriggle, climb and fall reflecting the human emotions onstage, but they never resolve. Indeed the entire opera never experiences a perfect cadence until the last page of the score. That's over four hours of making you wait for musical closure. There are no built-in buttons for applause anywhere in the score and you can usually judge the audience's approval by the length of silence before the applause starts at the final curtain. If it's a great performance, the applause can last almost as long as the show itself.

The opera's plot is straightforward. Those of us who are fans of daytime television soap operas will find the story quite normal. Others may need to be more generous with their acceptance. Here goes. Tristan has been brought up in the court of his uncle Marke, who happens to be King of Cornwall. In combat Tristan killed an Irish knight who was engaged to his cousin Isolde, daughter of the Irish king. During the combat, Tristan has been dangerously wounded and places himself under Isolde's care. Should we also know that Isolde comes of a race skilled in magic spells? She recognises him and nurses him to health, even though she is aware that he is her fiancé's killer. At the same time, she also develops a deep passion for him. The feeling becomes mutual but both deem their love unrequited. Soon after Tristan's return to Cornwall, he is dispatched to Ireland by King Marke that he may win Isolde for his queen. This all happens before the curtain goes up.

Our story opens on board the ship on which Tristan brings Isolde to Cornwall. An offstage tenor sailor sings of his wild Irish rose back home. 'Irische Maid' doesn't quite have the same feel when sung in the German language but this is one of the few moments when Wagner reminds us of the story's Irish origins.

What on earth convinced Richard Wagner to write an opera based on an Irish legend? There is a poem by Gottfried von Strassburg on the subject of *Tristan and Isolde* or *Tristram and Ysolt* (or Iseult or Ysonde) dating from about 1150. Wagner's attraction to plots that deal with gods, monsters, roaming ghosts, the Holy Grail, kings and knights is well known, yet, for some unknown reason, this plot took his fancy. Wagner's work on *Tristan und Isolde* was initiated when he set to music five poems by Mathilde Wesendonck, known as the *Wesendonck Lieder*. Two of those songs, 'Im Treibhaus' (In the Greenhouse) and 'Träume' (Dreams) were studies for the much larger and longer work that became *Tristan und Isolde*.

Deeming her love for Tristan unrequited, Isolde determines to end her sorrow by quaffing a death potion; and Tristan, feeling that the woman he loves is about to be wedded to another, readily consents to share it with her.

Isolde's mezzo-soprano companion, Brangäne, substitutes a love potion for the death draught and their love rises to almost overwhelming passion. Here Wagner gives us about 20 minutes of a love duet,. 'O sink hernieder, Nacht der Liebe, gib Vergessen' (Descend, o night of love and grant oblivion).

Not long after they reach Cornwall, they are surprised in the garden of the castle by the king and Tristan is severely wounded by Melot, one of King Marke's knights. Kurwenal, Tristan's faithful retainer, bears him to Kareol Castle. Isolde follows, arriving just in time to fold him in her arms as he dies. Over his corpse she sings the breathtakingly beautiful 'Liebestod' (Love death) and she dies too.

In the early decades of last century, two great Australian sopranos ventured the long role of Isolde in international houses. Florence Austral and Marjorie Lawrence both enjoyed enormous success and both suffered physical illness that quickly ended their careers. This had nothing to do with their Isolde performances. Austral (real name Florence Fawaz) found herself afflicted by multiple sclerosis and Lawrence's career took a rapid turn in 1941 when she contracted polio. Her public performance of Isolde two years after this debilitating illness was a feat of human endurance. As pictured in her film autobiography, *Interrupted Melody*, her Isolde appeared beautifully reclining on a rock or a chaise lounge only to drag her limp body over the dead Tristan to sing the 'Liebestod'. Her voice in the movie was dubbed by the fabulous American soprano, Eileen Farrell, although Lawrence also recorded a soundtrack that went unused. 'You need your legs to sing!' cackled one of her bitchy contemporaries. One thoughtless society patron tried her hand at complimenting Eileen Farrell. 'My dear, you reminded me so much of Kate Smith.' The well-loved Kate Smith was principally a radio singer and her figure was nothing like that of a model. Farrell's short frame was also 'healthy' and she was known for her direct, sometimes coarse, manner. On this occasion she immediately responded with 'Well, kiss my ass!' and stormed out.

There are some wonderful Farrell anecdotes,

most of them too crude for inclusion here. Farrell and another American soprano Beverly Sills were shopping between takes of their recording of Gaetano Donizetti's *Maria Stuarda*. While they were looking through some woollen tops a shop assistant asked the very buxom Farrell if she could help. 'Got anything big enough for these puppies?' Farrell asked, pointing at her impressive double Ds.

Farrell was the first American soprano to be associated with the title role of *Medea*. Luigi Cherubini's bluntly chilling opera, loosely based on the legend of Jason and the Golden Fleece, ends with the soprano killing both her children to stop them being taken by their father. At the dress rehearsal of a concert performance starring Farrell, the conductor decided to flaunt his ego from the podium to impress the invited audience. 'Darling, don't you think we should be a little softer here? The rise to the A flat should show more vengeance. Can we hold the pause a little longer?' The conductor continued in this vein, destroying any sense of flow and drama that the final rehearsal required. Farrell walked to the front of the stage and in her clearest and booming voice said, 'Honey, I don't tell you how to suck dick. Don't tell me how to sing!' There was a pregnant pause and then the rehearsal continued without even the suggestion of further advice from the conductor.

Oddly enough, Eileen Farrell's operatic career lasted less than a decade – not because her voice was unsuited to the repertoire but because she wasn't one to hold her tongue and accept the temperaments of the industry. Long before and long after her stage career, she performed opera in concert. Her Isolde was one that covered all expectations. If you're able to get hold of some of these recorded performances, conducted by Leonard Bernstein, they will convince you of the true worth of Wagner's masterpiece.

Like Brünnhilde's immolation scene, Isolde's 'Liebestod' is a summing up of her life's emotions. You can often hear it on orchestral concert programmes attached to the Vorspiel. In this type of performance it is played merely as an orchestral solo. Even without the soaring sound of the soprano, it is still a wonderful piece of musical emotion. In the opera's finale, Isolde sings 'Mild und leise wie er lächelt' (How softly and gently he smiles), starting with motif number 15, known as the Love in Death. It rises in sentiment as the orchestral forces become more passionate, ending with a rapturous 'höchste Lust!' (utmost rapture!) as the curtain slowly falls to a hushed silence from the audience.

Wagner's music theatre is like the most potent drug. Once you're hooked, there's no turning back.

THE PRIMA DONNA

PRIMA DONNAS ARE a very special breed of performer. The most famous are followed around the world by adoring fans and are usually known more for their onstage and offstage antics than for their vocal performances. Sure, a diva should be able to 'hit the notes' with some accuracy and the stage should light up whenever she comes on the stage, but it's what is talked about in the media that makes them important.

The first mistake for any performer is to believe one's own publicity. Norma Desmond in that legendary film *Sunset Boulevard* made that fatal mistake. If you believe the good reviews, you must also believe the bad ones. The truth is usually somewhere in between. Publicity encourages the audience's response to the performer and the diva soon learns that she can ask for almost anything she desires and it will almost magically appear. She becomes like a privileged, naughty child.

The bigger the celebrity, the larger the demands. If

you are fortunate enough to view a contract for a big-name performer you might note an amazing list of requests/demands called riders. These are necessary items that must be provided by the hirer to make the artist feel 'comfortable'. They may range in size from brand-named mineral water at a specific temperature (which will be listed in the contract) or fruit and teabags with hot water in the dressing room to larger necessities like the make and model of a chauffeured car they must have on call. One diva I know requires three adjoining apartments and stays in the middle one. She insists that this is so she can vocalise without disturbing her neighbours. Another star travels with most of her own furniture – and this is on international tours. That's real power. In the old days, Prima donnas used to have poodles. Now they have agents.

Once, conducting an outdoor concert series with a famous diva, I was shown to my dressing room, which was actually a tent. It had no floor, just grass, a table without a chair, a mirror and a clothes hanger – without any hangers. One has to make do in these situations. The orchestral members had similar lodgings. The soprano was housed in a two-roomed suite that had been brought to the venue complete with a fashionable lounge suite, bar and food of every kind at her disposal. Still, the audience had paid good money to see her.

Some years ago I was conducting a concert for a famous Korean soprano. The concert was sold out before being advertised, so strong is her following. I had been given the details of the programme and all seemed well until a few days before she arrived in the country. She called to advise that she had received a better offer and wanted to cancel the concert. The producers would not release her from the contract so, to allow her to do both gigs, she had organised to perform the programme without interval, then do the other concert.

The day before the concert the orchestra and I had one three-hour session to rehearse the 90-minute programme. That was it. The soprano arrived just as the rehearsal was about to begin and informed us that a television crew wanted to record two arias to be broadcast that evening. Without rehearsal we 'busked' these two arias for the waiting media. She then instructed me to trim any long instrumental introduction down to a few chords, in order to reduce the performance time. Any orchestral solo would have to be heavily cut. The 12-minute *William Tell* overture would start at the trumpet fanfare that heralds the final section of the well-known piece. That made it about two minutes long. A ravishingly beautiful Bellini aria *might* be shorn of its recitative, depending on how the time was going ... The first encore, a Korean national song, would only have one of its three verses. The arrangement of Victor Herbert's 'Italian Street Song' from *Naughty Marietta*, which I had spent hours writing would not be needed. The concert would be fast and slick.

The day came and I went into her dressing room to give the usual 'in bocca al lupo' (in the mouth of the wolf) greeting. She said sharply, 'You should be out there on the podium!' We still had ten minutes before starting. The performance began and she sang for her devoted audience like an angel. She was wonderful. Every time she appeared she was wearing a different gown and her fans soaked up every part of the show. Obviously she had miscalculated the exact length of the programme and, by the time we arrived at the encores, she decided to sing all three verses of the Korean song and the 'Italian Street Song'. Had we rehearsed it we would have immediately noticed that it was up a full tone from the key she liked... She and I got through it and, as we left the stage following numerous bows, she was pulled away by members of her entourage, who quickly ripped out her hair extensions and dressed her in readiness for the car that was awaiting her at the front of the theatre. She caught the 10.10 p.m. flight back to Korea, where she performed a few hours after landing.

The same soprano made news headlines when she left a production before the final performance and forgot to tell the management. Rumours quickly circulated that she was ill, pregnant, bored, didn't like the conductor. Ten days later she sang the same role in Rome, and she was perfectly fine. Was she chastised in any way for this behaviour? Her audience had come to see her and she had snubbed their devotion.

A male opera lover who is fascinated by sopranos is sometimes called an opera queen. That term really dates from the 1960s and is today somewhat passé, as the age of the diva seems to have passed. These opera queens thrive on knowing every aspect of their favourite soprano's life – her operatic roles, future operatic engagements, shopping preferences, foibles and private life. At times opera queens go as far as dressing up as their favourite diva. They might also join groups of like-minded fans to honour their star in group discussions. One can locate thousands of these groups on the worldwide web, but beware not to succumb to their evil. Without the opera queen, the prima donna would have been unable to survive. Had it not been for the OQ, Maria Callas and Renata Tebaldi would have been great friends rather than gossiped-about arch-rivals. Beverly Sills would have been less of a celebrity. Kathleen Battle would have been simply a charming soubrette.

Much has been written about the temperamental Kathleen Battle's unique personality. I can only retell a moment viewed from the back of an empty auditorium, in a discreet position, watching her rehearse an upcoming recital with her pianist. She stood in the bell of the piano going through her repertoire, eyes closed, lips lightly together, without making any vocal sound. The pianist was in deep concentration coping with some very technically difficult pages. Ms Battle did not seem to include him at all in her performance as she silently emoted. With a sudden turn, she stopped and glared at the pianist and said, 'Keep up!'

Of course, there is the young diva, the killer soprano, the kind who would walk over her dying grandmother to secure herself an operatic role or contract. Nothing will stand in her way, so tunnelled is her vision. This type of performer is seldom admired by her peers yet she frequently has an audience following. Having and maintaining a career is all-encompassing, the focus of her life. The young diva frequently uses her naivety to disarm her opponents. What immediately comes to mind is the typical back-handed compliment to a fellow performer following a concert: 'Do you know, my friends liked you – and they'd never heard of you before!' Is this a thoughtless comment or purposely said to deflate the opponent's ego? The killer soprano is a charmless performer who upstages everyone else. Her ego is what you see first, not her character or talent.

There is a handful of 'oddity' divas who require special mention. The most familiar was Florence Foster Jenkins, whose personal wealth enabled her to hire major auditoriums and sing whatever she liked. She had a huge cult following and her performances were sold out. Unfortunately her prima donna status was founded on the fact that she could not sing and, presumably, was unaware that the audiences were laughing *at* her. Her piano accompanist had the curious name of Cosme McMoon and his story is a book in itself.

Later a true diva emerged on the opera scene. Her name was Olive Middleton and she had a short but not splendid career in the early years of last century. In the early 1960s – yes, half a century later – she decided to start her own company run by the most typical Jewish princess, Madame La Puma, in New York. The La Puma Opera Company performed the great works of the repertoire – *Norma*, *La Gioconda*, *Tosca*, *Die Walküre*, *Aida*, *La Forza del Destino*, *Fedora* and *Andrea Chenier*. You name it, they did it. Olive Middleton was the reigning diva even though she was in her seventies. Though not a professional company, it had a great following from an audience that included many of the great names of the opera industry. The surviving recorded documents reveal the energy of the occasion. On these rare audio captures, Madame Middleton rarely sings a note on pitch (she rarely knows the details of the score) yet she receives enormous ovations after every great moment. In her mind she is very great artist and she tries to bring some of that stellar quality to her performances. The audience thrills to the stuffed owl she has attached to her arm while performing Norma. They cheer when she lunges for the top C (and misses it by a mile) in the 'Miserere' in *Il Trovatore*. Her realisation of Tosca is extraordinary. Will she die of old age before the final jump? I suspect that her daily medication included several verismo tablets. An elderly colleague told me that he'd asked Madame Middleton when they would be fortunate to experience her Donna Anna in *Don Giovanni* again. Her response was clear and adamant. 'I'm sorry my dear, the Elvira isn't quite up to it!'

In the 1980s, public access cable television in America enjoyed the regular broadcasts of Madame Mari Lyn, another wealthy widow who longed for vocal fame. She performed a variety of repertoire from simple songs to the grandest of arias accompanied by an instrumental quartet comprising two violins, a cello and a piano. She had little talent but a lot of money. Footage of her television presentations – complete with her heavy Brooklyn accent –is ideal party material. Better still is the little-known Portuguese soprano Natalia de Andrade whose voice is preserved on a very small handful of vanity records. (These are so named because they are financed in every way by the artist.) Madame Andrade excels every previous diva on record with her intense drama, her conviction and the lack of any vocal beauty.

Madame Vera Galupe-Borszkh is the last remaining great prima donna of the old school. In fact, to quote her biog, 'she was the only one still enrolled at that school'. Vera is the creation of the brilliant singer, vocal coach and opera director Ira Siff. With Madame Vera Galupe-Borszkh he reminds us, in an hilarious way, what a diva used to be. All the quirks – the ego, the simplicity of intelligence, the pouting, the hair – are there on grand display and lovingly delivered.

At home a diva can be quite simple. One, who now lives in retirement, has a television, tuned to the shopping channel, in every room in her house, just in case she misses anything she'd like to buy! Another was dining at my home when suddenly, mid-meal and mid-conversation, she exclaimed, 'It's 8.30. Time for *The Brady Bunch Exposed*.' We had to leave the table and watch television for an hour in absolute silence, while she absorbed the special exposé edition of her favourite television programme. Do you know how many divas watch daily soap operas? The answer would astound you.

TOSCA

YOU'D THINK THAT, by the time an artist is contracted for a fabulous leading role like Tosca in Puccini's great musical drama from 1900, the celebrity soprano might have accepted her God-given talents and be at one with herself. How wrong can you be? The greater celebrity an artist holds, the more insecure they usually are about their talents. That's why conductors, directors, music staff and stage crew expect to handle them with kid gloves from the first day of rehearsals. Of course, it's the end result of the performances that we see as the light at the end of the tunnel so it's best to keep the soprano happy until that deadline. After that, the roller-coaster ride of performances seems quite easy.

Presumably the soprano knows what the role requires musically and theatrically as the production period begins. She'll certainly be aware that the audience expects a star performance. You simply cannot do *Tosca* without a star turn. No ticket buyer will accept it, and why should they? Puccini tailor-made his operatic characters for the greatest singing actors of the time. *Tosca* is verismo at its best. Without that theatrical essence, the character loses so much of its operatic appeal. From the earliest days, *Tosca* has been on the Top 10 list of best-loved operas. It shows what the art form is all about.

Picture this ... When you go to see *Tosca* in the theatre, the soprano mostly looks like a typical soprano. She has glamour. She's quite attractive (courtesy of several hours with the make-up artist) and you can believe that she's an opera singer which Tosca certainly is. Her lover Cavaradossi, the tenor, is very much the antithesis of a gay icon. He's frequently a short podgy fellow with an undetectable toupee, that hairpiece affectionately known as a rug. If you look not too hard you'll probably see a rather high heel built into his shoes. That part of his costume looks like a leftover from the television series *Lost in Space*. On the other hand, the bad guy baritone Scarpia is almost always tall with matinée idol looks, incredibly opinionated and wearing very, very tight trousers. Some of the Toscas with whom I've worked should really think themselves lucky.

Most operas include a death somewhere in the show to make the story more exciting and, by *Tosca*'s final curtain, all three leads have died – sometimes along with some of the audience members. That's a 60 per cent death rate.

The first death happens very quickly (as some deaths do) with a lightning fast idea that comes to Tosca as she ponders her fate in Act Two. 'Do I give myself up to the Roman Chief of Police to enable my lover, a painter turned activist, to fake his own death at a dummy execution?' That's a rather big question for a soprano.

While Tosca considers her options, Puccini gets her to sing an aria 'Vissi d'arte' (I have lived for art), asking God why He's making all this happen to her. After all, she's been a good girl bringing flowers to the altar every day, singing for free in the church etc. She's lived her life for her art and her love (one Hungarian Tosca I know lived her life for cleanliness and was discovered on her hands and knees scrubbing the bath in her dressing room before a performance) and she's never hurt a living soul. It takes Tosca only about three minutes after her famous aria to learn how to kill. At a good performance, as she wields the knife, it's like she's auditioning for *Scream 4*. At that rather violent moment Tosca repeatedly stabs Scarpia, while singing her lines in time with the conductor's beat.

Tosca is an opera in three acts but really it's a one-act opera with an epilogue and coda. Everything of importance to the story happens in that middle act. Act One introduces the three main characters, and we find out a couple of dramatically important points. Floria Tosca is, by profession, a singer of some renown. She's in love with the painter Mario Cavaradossi who has a secret life as a political activist. Baron Scarpia is Chief of Police and corrupt to the core. Like some other famous operatic characters we will meet later in this book, he fancies the ladies and currently has his sights on our Tosca. He suspects Cavaradossi to be party to the political strife and thinks he can kill two birds with one stone by seducing Tosca. That's basically what we learn in the prologue, otherwise known as Act One. After the interval the real action begins.

The onstage action of Act Two happens in Scarpia's apartment in the Farnese Palace. He's having dinner while Cavaradossi is in the torture chamber next door. In actual fact the tenor is standing in the wings in prompt corner with his music score on a lighted stand, his offstage cries and screams being cued by an assistant conductor. Without this important person, who momentarily replaces the 'real' conductor, the musical accuracy might delve into new realms of fantasy. In the other corner of the room is a window through which the strains (I'll leave that one alone) of Tosca's singing over a choral cantata waft in. Scarpia and his henchmen sing some dialogue over this offstage sound and, as the soprano sustains a high C from the wings, he closes the window, thus ending the note mid-flight. It's an effective theatrical moment. A minute later the diva herself enters in her best, most glamorous attire. When you visualise a Tosca, she's usually in this costume with boobs for days. There's some small talk, then Cavaradossi screams in pain from the torture chamber. Tosca gets down to the job of saving her lover.

After some struggling with Scarpia, and a brilliant trio with Cavaradossi, jubilant that his cause has hit a home run, Tosca asks Scarpia 'Quanto?' (How much?)

'Quanto?' he responds, knowing full well that he'll have to explain the obvious to the soprano.

This is a tricky moment for Tosca but she accepts Scarpia's offer to mount a dummy execution for the dummy tenor if she gives her all to him (and some Toscas have a lot of all). Scarpia writes a letter of pardon for Cavaradossi then comes towards Tosca ready for the big embrace. This is when the stabbing occurs.

One of Australia's finest and best-loved sopranos, Maureen Howard, debuted at a very young age with the role of Tosca. She started at the top. A performance in Canberra in the late 1960s contained a most curious moment for all onlookers. Her Hungarian-born Scarpia, Alexander Major, a great voice but rather lacking in stage awareness, managed to die exactly where the curtain landed ending Act Two. The charming and stage-wise Maureen Howard placed the candles – important to the stage action – in positions that would not catch the curtain as it descended. The stage manager's foresight enabled the old-fashioned hand-pulled curtain to be pushed forward by a stagehand. Unfortunately, the curtain had to be tugged by the stagehand in order for it to rise again immediately for the picture call (this is when the curtain is raised to reveal the final scene again, with the cast frozen like a picture snapshot). The young sprite clung too hard and went with the curtain as it ascended, his legs dangling below the proscenium arch while the 'foul-mouthed' Tosca (her description) yelled profanities at the Scarpia as he sat up from the dead position saying 'What's going on?' Many years later, that stagehand with the dangling legs became artistic director of a major opera company.

The action of Act Three is placed on the battlements of the Castel Sant'Angelo in Rome. Following the tenor's big aria, which is usually followed by long applause, Tosca runs in to give him the good news that he's not going to die. He's going to act dead. At a rehearsal, one great celebrity soprano ran onstage at this moment without the rather beautiful brown cape that she threw over the glitzy gown from Act Two. The director stopped the rehearsal and quietly said over the microphone from the auditorium 'Darling, where's your cape?' If he looked a few feet to her left he'd have seen her ashen-faced personal dresser holding the apparel. 'It's brown,' the soprano complained in her broad Southern American accent. She had endured several costume fittings and had known for weeks the colour combinations of her gowns but decided, on this day, that she'd refuse to wear it. 'Darling,' the director went on, 'the cape is a beautiful brown hue that perfectly suits the diva. Tosca's a diva.' She retorted, 'Honey, I'm a diva and I don't wear *no brown.*' What could be said? By opening night she was wearing the brown.

The Australian tenor Lance Ingram who made his international career and base in France, with his name changed to Albert Lance, experienced an unnecessary goof-up at the Old Theatre Royal in Sydney in the late 1950s. The production arrived in town but the prop rifles for the soldiers in Act Three could not be found. The aged theatre manager remembered that he had some in the basement. Unfortunately the dusty old rifles were stocked with wads rather than the blanks that are compulsory for safely regulations. Lance received six real gunshots and fell to the ground with blood pouring out of his torso, crying out, 'I've been bloody shot!' Did that show on the surtitles – or did the audience understand the situation?

The late super-celebrity tenor Luciano Pavarotti retired from operatic work with the role of Cavaradossi. His less than slim proportions and back problems didn't allow him to collapse naturally when he was executed. It took a good two minutes to arrange the conveniently placed pillows to form a bed for his 'dead' body. If this wasn't enough to warrant disbelief from theatrical illusion, he managed to drink a full glass of water while his Tosca was pouring out her love in the Act One duet. What conceit for the art of opera and the paying audience, let alone the stage drama.

One of my early attempts to learn from a

conductor of authority came in the first year of my professional working life. A quite eccentric Italian conductor, Carlo Felice Cillario, then in the autumn of his life, was a regular visitor to the national company. I sought his advice on many matters relating to the repertoire I loved and I was fortunate that he was so generous with his time. Over several months we spent many hours combing through a handful of scores that would put me in good stead for my own career on the podium. Perhaps the most vital information he passed to me was when studying the score and text of *Tosca*. I knew very well that he had conducted many celebrity casts in this particular work, especially Maria Callas. In fact, Carlo had conducted her final performances in the role, sadly her last operatic staged appearances. When I conducted my first *Tosca* many years later, I had the strangest feeling that the spirits of opera past were with me on the podium, supporting me and the cast through this sensational work. I was proud to boast to the orchestra and cast that we'd be playing from Carlo's orchestral score and parts, which had been used in the pit when Callas, Tito Gobbi, Regine Crespin, Leonie Rysanek and Franco Corelli sang! I hope those ghosts were happy with our performances.

LUCIA DI LAMMERMOOR

WHEN MOST PEOPLE think of opera, preconceived images come to mind. There's the fat lady with the horned helmet who sings Wagner, the powder-wigged gentry of the Mozart repertoire and there's the lady running about the stage in her bloodied nightie having gone mad and stabbed her bridegroom – poor Scottish lass that she is.

Unlike most of the great works of the operatic repertoire, *Lucia di Lammermoor* was a success right from the start. Its composer, Gaetano Donizetti noted that the first-night audience 'listened in religious silence and then hailed with spontaneous cheers'. That was 26 September 1835 at the Teatro San Carlo in Naples. In some of the performance I've witnessed, the 'religious silence' could have been called sleep. At the first *Lucia di Lammermoor* performances I attended, the man a couple of seats from me had a lovely doze throughout the entire mad scene, which is supposed to be the highlight of the opera. Even though the story can be dramatically convincing, the opera itself requires at least four excellent singing actors cast in the principal roles to make it really accessible to a modern audience.

The published work of the Scottish poet and novelist Sir Walter Scott (1771–1832) inspired a generation of Italian and French composers. Rossini's *La Donna del Lago* was based on Scott's poem, 'The Lady of the Lake'. Georges Bizet set Scott's novel *'The Fair Maid of Perth* as *La Jolie Fille de Perth*, an unjustly neglected opera. Six years before setting Scott's novel *'The Bride of Lammermoor'*, Donizetti had composed *Elisabetta al Castello di Kenilworth* but created his best and most popular work with *Lucia di Lammermoor*. In the same decade, at least five other respected composers set Scott's story of Lucy with varying success – Adam, Carafa, Rieschi, Bredal and Mazzucata – but Donizetti's version eclipsed them all! The main reason you go to see this opera is that it features a celebrity name in the title role. Lucia is a role many sopranos have used to make their names. After almost a decade of stupendous singing in various standard and contemporary roles, Joan Sutherland achieved overnight fame singing Donizetti's heroine at the Royal Opera House, Covent Garden. She then used Lucia as a calling card in the other big houses in New York, Paris and Milan, and sang her for another three decades.

Before Sutherland, Maria Callas had placed her

particular stamp on the role and the world was reintroduced to the glories of the bel canto repertoire. High birdlike sopranos had performed the title role from the beginning of last century – particularly Luisa Tetrazzini, Amelita Galli-Curci and Lily Pons – but with Callas's exceptional voice and incredible connection to the drama and character, thoughts changed. Suddenly audiences were presented with real-life drama rather than pretty singing from chubby ladies. That's really what bel canto is – the perfect combination of singing (beautiful singing with long lines injected with emotion) and acting. Callas did all that and set the benchmark for all those who followed.

Before we get on with the plot, I must declare that Donizetti was very fortunate to have the services of Salvatore Cammarano as his librettist. The text is so good that you could perform it as a straight play. Cammarano manages to omit a lot of the unnecessary 'Scottish' detail that Sir Walter Scott favoured and, set to the vocal lines of Donizetti, the opera becomes the quintessential Italian opera.

There's a mild curiosity with the character's names in the opera. Cammarano has Italianised them to allow the singers to vocalise the Italian vowels. Therefore, Henry becomes Enrico, Edgar is Edgardo, Raymond is Raimondo etc. Lucy's name ends with an 'a' because she's a girl. If that's not confusing enough, they keep their Scottish surnames. Listen to Lucia in her first scene referring to Ravenswood. It sounds as foreign as a well-known tenor singing 'Ahm drehmeen av a whaeet Cheesstmahss'.

The musical score brims with dramatic and melodic delights. The sombre chords that open the opera suggest both the mist-covered hills and imminent doom of our two leads. I hate it when directors 'produce' a visual effect on stage at this moment rather than letting Donizetti do it with the music. It's as though they don't trust the score. Once I had to endure the chorus re-enacting the funeral of Lucia's mother during these few pages. Choristers are not admired for their quiet footwork, especially during soft music.

A brass fanfare heralds the start of the action and we're suddenly 40 miles north of Edinburgh (the county of Sir Walter Scott) in about 1700. This is one opera it's hard to modernise to Mars in 2070. It simply doesn't work. The plot opens with problems afoot between the Ravenswood and Ashton clans, whose rivalry resembles that of the Montagues and Capulets. Lucia Ashton is currently dating Edgardo di Ravenswood. Her brother Enrico wants her to marry Lord Arturo Bucklaw (yes, his real Christian name is Arthur) and he deceives her into believing that Edgardo has been unfaithful. You've probably worked out that the brother is a baddy and, hence, a baritone. The gentlemen of the chorus, along with a character tenor Normanno (who needs to be a singer with a really loud voice because the orchestra usually drowns out all his solos), are outside the castle. They are joined by Raimondo the priest and Lucia's brother Enrico, who sings an aria about how he hates Edgardo (not just because he's getting a higher fee for the performance). He then bursts into a testosterone-filled cabaletta reinforcing his plight, joined by the chorus.

After mild applause, because it's only ten minutes into the show and the fat lady hasn't sung, we are shown into the garden. There's a tinkling fountain that makes the audience feel uneasy if they didn't visit the bathroom before the curtain went up. After some majestic orchestral chords there's a harp solo as Lucia wanders around inspecting the scenery. Clearly, Donizetti was very particular when writing for solo instruments in his operas. The sound of the harp suggests purity. Later in the score he uses the flute to show Lucia's madness.

Alone with her maid Alisa (the mezzo), Lucia relates the ghost legend of the fountain. 'Regnava nel silenzio' (Silence over all was reigning) is an entrance aria that lets us know that she's loopy. To strengthen this idea, Lucia bursts forth with a cabaletta about how happy she is when Edgardo is around. As he has been summoned, he arrives for a secret rendezvous. Alisa mutters that she will keep watch and leaves. Edgardo looks like a tenor but, wearing the traditional Scottish kilt, he appears even shorter. Together he and Lucia sing a duet where they take a solemn vow to marry and exchange rings.

We are in Enrico's bedroom (or library) for the start of Act Two. He tells Lucia absolute lies – like the one about the Ashton guy who has been fooling around with a female stage manager, or some other attractive person in the wings. There's a wonderful scene which includes a three-part duet. The first is full of coloratura for soprano and baritone followed by a sad slow middle part. Offstage horns are heard, which prompt them to sing the fast finale. Now the boring bit happens – the bass enters to perform his scene with Lucia. Sometimes this entire scene is cut even though it includes pages of fine music. The problem is, what can you do dramatically with a priest who's a bass? Sure enough, Raimondo convinces Lucia to go against her heart and agree to marry Arturo, the second tenor.

The second scene of Act Two is set at the lavish wedding ceremony for Lucia and Arturo. There's an opening chorus and some dancing (ballet dancers in kilts) and Arturo sings his arietta (that's a short aria). Enrico announces Lucia's arrival. Why should he? We can see that she's the only one in a wedding dress. She's almost fainting and being supported by the 'friendly' Raimondo. As she feebly agrees to sign the wedding contract, Edgardo, whom we haven't seen for over half an hour, jumps in with a lot of questions. Of course, this is an excellent chance to sing the famous *Lucia* sextet. Actually it's a quartet with Alisa and Arturo singing along. The chorus also joins in at the end, so it's a mammoth ensemble. The audience generally likes this number no matter how it is sung. Edgardo rants, raves and throws his ring back at Lucia. She faints and it's time for an interval.

The second half of the performance usually opens with the festivities of the wedding night but Donizetti and Cammarano wrote the rather great Wolf's Crag scene for the tenor and baritone which should begin the Act. In this Edgardo challenges Enrico to a duel to be fought near the tombs of the Ravenswoods. The scene opens with loud cracking of thunder, hopefully to drown out the orchestra, and finishes with a splendid martial duet for tenor and baritone.

After a brief scene change we're back at the wedding party with more ballet dancing. Towering over the assembled guests, Raimondo announces that there's been an incident. In an aria, he tells us that Lucia has forgotten to take her medication and managed to stab her new husband on the wedding night. ('He ran into my knife ten times!' she later told the police.) They all sing about how sad it makes them feel. The reception food wasn't great anyway.

Lucia enters with eyes glazed over. What occurs now is one of the greatest 'show numbers' for a soprano and probably the most famous mad scene in all opera. Donizetti incorporates a flute obbligato, which flits around the voice and echoes almost everything Lucia sings. Originally, Donizetti tried the glass harmonica as the obbligato instrument. A glass harmonica is a collection of different-sized wineglasses that make a pitched noise when you run a damp finger over the rim (similar to the sound you accidentally make when you're listening to a boring conversation at the bar). Because of the temperamental nature of the glass harmonica (i.e. the liquid may evaporate when exposed to heat and alter the pitch when played), Donizetti decided it would be better to cast a flute instead.

At the end of the first part of the mad scene, Donizetti requested the flute and soprano to improvise a cadenza. This is a virtuosic passage sung by the soprano and joined by the flute in a 'free' rhythmic style. For many generations, standard cadenzas have been used at this point but I find it thrilling to hear new ideas. Why should every singer use the same cadenza? It is supposed to be an extension of the drama and the personality of the artist. I was attacked by critics once for writing my own cadenza for this scene which used two flutes. Lucia had a wonderfully mad time buzzing around with both instruments, and the audience loved it. Frequently the cadenza recalls the tunes of Lucia and Edgardo's duet or the duet she has with Enrico. At any rate, she ends up on a high E flat and has a mild collapse. This is not yet the end of her role, however, as she has yet to sing the cabaletta, which also ends on a sustained high E flat. Some sopranos transpose the entire scene up a full tone and end on a really high F. That was

Donizetti's original conception. Lucia collapses and dies. Usually there's a lot of applause at this point. Sir Walter Scott's novel had dear Lucy dying some time later but Donizetti and his librettist thought that audiences would appreciate seeing the whole spectacle in one evening.

I was preparing a production several years ago where the celebrity prima donna was to arrive a few days before opening. She had an understudy but she was also rehearsing Gilda in *Rigoletto* and was tied up with those rehearsals. To fill the gaps in our *Lucia di Lammermoor* rehearsals the director placed himself as the understudy. We didn't mind because it saved us singing and embarrassing ourselves. The only trouble was that the contracted Korean soprano was petite and the rehearsal director was a balding middle-aged fellow with a rotund physique. Can you picture him running to the table and placing the lace tablecloth over his head as he sang the mad scene? It wasn't a pretty sight. His singing voice made me tastefully suggest that, if Donizetti had heard his particular sound, he'd have written the flute obbligato for a lawn mower. Oddly enough, this suggestion was not taken as a compliment.

We have one more scene before the opera's over.

Remember Edgardo? He's alone in the Ravenswood cemetery waiting for the duel to take place, knowing nothing of the news of last night. He sings a divine aria, 'Fra poco a me ricovero, darà negletto avello' (Some forgotten grave will soon give me shelter). The gentlemen of the chorus come in with Raimondo and tell Edgardo that there's not going to be any duel – Lucia's dead. In the original Scott novel, Edgar loses himself on the seashore and is drowned but here, in the opera version, he plunges a dagger into his breast and sings an aria about the joys of being reunited with Lucia in heaven.

That's the joy of Italian opera. You can usually die going out on a high note.

LA TRAVIATA

MY FIRST TRIP to Italy was memorable. Rather than the usual operatic haunts in Rome or Milan, I made a beeline for Venice to spend time with a rather eccentric musicologist guru who was to make me think in quite a different light about certain aspects of the opera repertoire. His unique ideas, specifically on tempi, were based on the astrological planets and their corresponding star signs that greatly influenced George Frederic Handel, Johann Hasse and like composers. He spoke at great length about Martian and Venusian speeds and how they correlated precisely with modern-day metronome markings. Mars was the God of War and his tempo was a definite march. Venus, God of Love, had more of a waltz tempo. This was the tip of the iceberg. His other concepts included engaging the forces of a modern-sized symphony orchestra for the performance of baroque repertoire. This might sound extreme but his documentary proof, held at his palazzo situated on the bend in the Grand

Canal, included the account books of the producers from Handel's day. Sure enough, they frequently had orchestras with 140 players.

His theories initially surprised me – shocked might be the more appropriate description – but I came home convinced that he certainly had unearthed something of immense importance. He also had strong views on the attention spans of modern audiences and firmly believed that if the first act of an opera lasted longer than one hour something important – a new character entering, a set change, a dramatic or comedic shift – had to occur. This provided the audience with a kick to last the duration of the act.

I thought – and still think – that this is a great theory!

That Venetian visit also remained in my memory because I had the opportunity to visit the historic Teatro la Fenice (The Phoenix). As I was honoured with a private tour of Fenice's jewel box auditorium by the intendant (the general manager) I thought of the handful of great operas that had premiered in this theatre – above all, the two from Giuseppe Verdi's middle period: *Rigoletto* and *La Traviata*. Their tunes had soared into that auditorium and all the 'great' singers I'd read about had identified with their well-drawn characters. Though Gilda in *Rigoletto* is a gift of a role for almost any type of soprano, the role that sopranos kill for is Violetta in *La Traviata* or 'The Woman who has been Led Astray'.

The opera is based on the play, *La Dame aux Camélias,* by Alexandre Dumas fils. The action is set in France. Party girl Violetta Valéry meets a young suitor Alfredo Germont and they hook up. After living together just outside Paris for a couple of months Violetta is visited by Alfredo's father, Giorgio Germont. In a splendid scene which forms the centrepoint of the opera Germont asks Violetta to leave the relationship because it will bring a bad name to the family – and Alfredo's sister is soon to be wed and doesn't want any nastiness. Because she's nice, Violetta leaves Alfredo only to meet him again at a party held by Flora, another party girl. Alfredo denounces Violetta in front of the crowd and she faints. The final scene finds Violetta back in her old house, terminally ill with consumption. She reads a letter from Giorgio Germont, apologising for his mistaken actions. Alfredo returns, as does his father, just in time to see Violetta take her final breath.

History relates that the premiere of *La Traviata*, at Teatro la Fenice on 6 March 1853, was not a success because it had been performed in 'modern dress'. If only the critics had looked into the crystal ball to see what a 21st century 'concept' production would offer Verdi and Francesco Maria Piave (the librettist). We've had Violetta dying in hospital of an HIV-related illness, a wonderfully comedic Russian/Jewish Violetta who sniffs cocaine and keeps Alfredo's Y-fronts in her bedside box along with his father's letter, and a rather violent production where Alfredo's father rapes Violetta. Would the audience of 1853 have found these production ideas offensive?

I first worked in a production of *La Traviata* as a rehearsal pianist. The production was rather boring and the set featured a giant camellia flower hanging above the action. It did nothing more than sit there while the singers strutted their stuff underneath. The first time I conducted the opera, the design included a huge camellia on the proscenium arch, rather like a flower in a suit lapel. I remember emailing old friends about the production and mentioning the camellia. Their response was to ask if it looked like the camellia worn by Adelina Patti in the portrait above their mantelpiece. What I didn't expect was that my friends owned *the* Patti portrait that features in almost every book about the legendary diva. In fact, the flower holds an important message in the plot of the opera. In the first act, Alfredo asks when he can see Violetta again. She gives him a camellia and tells him to return when the flower has died. This was a clever way to say that it was her 'time of the month' and she'd be ready to welcome him back in a few days. In the 1970s, Londoners were gobsmacked when the Spanish soprano Montserrat Caballé sang the role and brought along her own Violetta costumes. Strangely enough, her Act Three costume was covered with red flowers! I doubt that anyone explained to Madame Caballé what the problem was.

One of the most terrifying moments for me came during a stage rehearsal for the first act. It was a spiffy new production set around 1890. The costumes looked great and the sets for each act were the finest and most detailed I've seen. It was very 'filmic' in its direction and the curtain – rather than the usual top to floor or side to centre variety – was like a camera iris that opened and closed from the middle of the stage. Following Verdi's orchestral prelude, there's busy laughter from the stage as Violetta's guests arrive for a party. The soprano arrives and sings a welcome to her friends and is introduced to the young gentleman called Alfredo. She immediately likes him and he invites her to join him in the famous 'Brindisi' (drinking song). He sings one verse then she enlivens the proceedings with the second verse. The duet ends on a high note from soprano and tenor, supported by the raised voices of everyone on stage. A soon as the applause thins there's an offstage group of musicians, supposedly from an adjoining room playing a fast waltz.

That's where my nightmare started. The day of the first major stage rehearsal I worked with the group of a dozen or so woodwind and brass players at 11 a.m. for an hour to rehearse them into the score. As they're offstage, they need to be available only for the times when they actually play. No costume is required or even direct contact with the main conductor. They had to follow my directions and I followed the conductor on the television monitor as we were hidden from audience view. Many musicians, especially brass players, are notorious for wanting to do the least amount of work followed by the most relaxation time. I had mistaken the starting time for the afternoon call and, instead of having two hours between rehearsals, we had only one hour. Of course, I didn't realise this until we received our call to the stage at 1 p.m. Where were the offstage band players? They had left the building for a nice boozy lunch at the local hotel. Stage management was making hasty phone calls to the hotel in desperation whilst I rapidly saw my life draw to a close in time to Verdi's score.

The Italian maestro was not noted for his slow tempi and the prelude and 'Brindisi' flew past in a few minutes. In the final measures of the latter I looked at the assembled musicians I had to conduct - an oboe, a second flute and a third horn. None of these instruments actually play the tune. I gave a very clear upbeat and they delivered a very feeble version of what was expected. The conductor stopped and growled something to the effect of 'Is too soft'. The great thing about this initial stage rehearsal is that it's also for getting the right positions for offstage things like this band. Dutifully I came onstage and asked him to repeat his criticism. 'Okay. Can we try again but I'll move the musicians a little closer to the front?' This filled in a few minutes while another two or three inebriated brass players rejoined the team. We tried again from the end of the 'Brindisi'. Again the maestro stopped. 'Is still too soft.' I repeated my act and asked for a couple of minutes while we moved the troupe forward. In the wings, the full crew had stumbled their way from the hotel to the rehearsal, ready to deliver. This time we sailed through the reading. I had survived, they had survived, the conductor was content and, most importantly, he never knew what was going on behind the wings.

Actually this incident was not as bad as a matinée performance of the same composer's *Otello*. Some members of the Act Two band – oboes and guitars – forgot that a matinée performance begins at 1 p.m. I had the honour of leading one oboe and a second guitar as the performance almost came to a halt. I clearly remember leaving the theatre as the remaining members of the offstage band entered through the stage door.

My debut *La Traviata* on the podium brought its own set of problems. I'd cast a rather lovely-looking soprano as Violetta. She had preceded this role with two of the four soprano roles in *The Tales of Hoffmann* and the title role in *Norma*. Her Violetta was a much anticipated event. Unfortunately she had performed the role in her student days and decided that this was the version she would play no matter what the director, conductor or other cast members did. She refused to vocalise until there was a paying audience in the theatre. This did not please her colleagues. She would not look at me or follow my direction on the podium, nor would she have any physical contact with her Alfredo, who was being performed by a very good-looking young tenor. Physical embraces became triangular stances and kisses were not even suggested. Need I say that the cast was not united? The director's worst nightmare came when she refused to perform Act Four (really Act Three because Act Two is in two scenes) with bare feet. She insisted on wearing stilettos and stockings, even though she's dying in bed. Her excuse? The floor was too cold. Those of you who have had even the briefest time on a performing stage will know how warm everything gets under lights. On the other hand, the soprano looked in amazement as the director, himself a famous 'transvesti' Violetta in an internationally adored all-male opera company sang all her cues at pitch, with the correct dramatic intention – something *she* never achieved.

It's extraordinary how mere gossip can become historical reality. In 1965 the soprano Joan Sutherland made a victorious homecoming after 15 years abroad. It was an historic moment in the history of opera in Australia. Over the span of a couple of months she sang many performances of five roles, including Violetta. Her Alfredos were shared principally by the American tenor John Alexander and a young Italian new to the scene called Luciano Pavarotti. The artists portraying

Giorgio Germont included the great baritone Robert Allman. A moment from his first performance went down in the annals of famous bloopers and has been detailed in several biographies of Sutherland.

The moment came in the scene in Flora's apartment just after Alfredo has thrown his gambling winnings in Violetta's face. Germont makes a spectacular entrance – all action comes to a halt – and he sings the dramatic phrase 'Di sprezzo degno' (For any man who offends a woman like that), enveloping the stage with his vocal power. At this particular performance the action and music paused in readiness for this phrase. All was silence. Nothing happened. The prompter cued then repeated the cue. Again nothing happened. Now the prompter spat out the words in loud clear tones: 'Di sprezzo degno'. After a few more death-defying moments of silence the Germont sang the word 'Cortigiani', the first word of the great aria of *Rigoletto*. Pandemonium broke forth and the cast somehow went on with tears of laughter in their eyes. In actual fact, as the surviving pirate recording of the performance confirms, this never happened. The true version is much simpler. Robert Allman merely reversed 'Di sprezzo degno' with the following phrase 'Se stesso rende'. There was not too much of a pause while he wracked his brain for the line and the audience would never have known of any problem. Sometimes I like to correct history.

Years later, in 1979, Sutherland was performing Elettra in Mozart's *Idomeneo* when almost every other member of the cast came down with an illness. Rather than cancel the performance the company decided to present *La Traviata* for one single night. The cast had not performed the opera for several years and would do their roles without benefit of rehearsal. This included the orchestra and chorus. Robert Allman, who had been Sutherland's principal baritone when she sang in her home country, sang up a storm in his old role. For obvious reasons, the performance that night had a rarely found electricity. All was breezing along in Act One with the entire cast on their toes remembering the words, music and directions from several years before. At the end of this act Violetta is left alone after her guests depart singing a fast noisy chorus. Reflecting on what has happened, she sings the big scena where she wonders if she should follow her instinct and spend more time with this new cute guy, Alfredo. She flings discretion to the wind and sings the brilliant cabaletta 'Sempre libera' (Always free). Alfredo's offstage singing interrupts her thoughts and she repeats the cabaletta, this time with more energy. This was Joan Sutherland's big moment but, for some unknown reason, she had a brief memory lapse and got lost. No matter. She called on her decades of experience with melodic ornamentation and improvised the most ravishing scales, moving around the harmonic progressions of the orchestra.

She even capped it off with a magnificent high E flat. This small mishap was turned into a fabulous display of vocal brilliance seldom heard in the theatre. That's what I call a diva with enterprise.

Celebrity divas portraying the role of Violetta are usually a joy. Caballé's need to wear her own costumes, no matter how glaringly they clashed with the production, is only the tip of the iceberg. The divine Anna Moffo, who was as beautiful in voice as she was in looks, had a production mounted for her at the Metropolitan Opera in New York in the mid-1960s. Cecil Beaton designed the sets and costumes around her personality and she performed the role in that house many times. The only problem was that she would faint somewhere during the performance, pausing the show while a doctor, or a replacement soprano, was found. Audiences would bet how far she would go in the opera each night before collapsing in a heap. One wonders if this was a deliberate call for audience sympathy (yes, it has been known to occur in the theatre) or that the soprano's petite figure could not cope with the physical demands of an operatic career.

One of the greatest Violettas of the 1950s and early 1960s, Romanian soprano Virginia Zeani, used Nellie Melba's Violetta fan to bring her luck. It did. In the previous century Adelina Patti was a great exponent of the role but her vocal score was so heavily cut it should have been advertised as 'Scenes from *La Traviata*'. I often wondered how the Royal Opera Covent Garden could perform *Fidelio* and *La Sonnambula* on one night – and that's with a ballet between the two works. Obviously they used Patti's scores.

In recent times, the American celebrity soprano Renée Fleming came in for much criticism for her overly dramatic reading of Violetta's 'Teneste la promessa' (you kept your promise), the letter she recites before singing her 'Farewell to life' aria in the final act. Annina, the maid, and Doctor Grenvil have left Violetta alone in her bed. She reaches under her pillow and produces the letter from Giorgio Germont. The strings shimmer and a solo violin plays the love theme that was originally sung by Alfredo. In a supposedly natural speaking voice, as dictated by Verdi, she reads the words: 'You have kept your promise. The duel took place. The baron was wounded but is recovering... etc...Alfredo is returning to you.' She peaks with the word 'curatevi' (Take care), then shakes her head with 'E tardi!' (Too late!). Violetta knows she has only a few more pages to sing before she dies. I've seen opera queens sit in the audience mouthing the words, a bit like a sing-a-long *The Sound of Music* or *The Rocky Horror Picture Show*. Somehow Renée Fleming, the darling of the record companies, chose the *Rocky Horror* as the template for her interpretation. Talk about over the top – a silent-screen actor would have been more dramatically restrained. Opera queens were jumping with glee.

A wonderful story told to me by an old conductor is verified by a recording of the performance. It occurred when Montserrat Caballé included 'Teneste la promessa' in a concert. The orchestra started, followed by the solo violin and 'Montsy' began her letter-reading. Now the trick is that the soprano must keep her ear to the key of the supporting orchestra while speaking the dialogue. When she gets to 'E tardi', which is usually quite riddled with sorrow, Violetta sings her next line and the remainder of the aria on Verdi's specified pitch. 'Montsy' got a bit carried away with the drama and started her sung phrase on a totally unrelated pitch. It sounded like Schoenberg. Realising that she'd taken the wrong road and unable to correct herself, what did she do? She took a page out of Anna Moffo's book and fainted! That'll always do it. A collapsing soprano always gets the sympathy of the audience.

An audience has to believe what it sees on stage. This is not to say that the performers should look exactly like their characters. Some artists of repute have not looked consumptive. Early last century Luisa Tetrazzini was revered as the definitive Violetta yet one could hardly imagine her dying of that particular medical condition in the final scene. Maria Callas sang the role before and after her tremendous weight loss. She sang it better before but looked perfect after. Giorgio Germont should be performed by an artist of a good vintage. I was lucky enough to conduct a 74-year-old baritone who had sung the role with Richard Tucker as his Alfredo. With his opening phrase 'Madamigella Valéry' he brought a wealth of experience onstage. He also sang like a god and stole the show every time.

A star role like Violetta needs much more than a soprano who can sing the notes and act the role. She needs to bring her career onstage with her, much as that old baritone did. She has to be a diva. It's that simple.

THE MEZZO
SOPRANO

THE SINGERS WHO draw the short straw in life are called mezzo sopranos. It's a sad but true fact. For the most part, composers wrote the most brilliant, the most sympathetic audience favourite roles for the soprano voice. Whether they be age, beauty or weight challenged, sopranos are always going to get the best parts and the best music to sing – and usually more money.

The mezzo is the female voice-type halfway between soprano and contralto. I get frustrated when an artist is in the concert programme listed as an alto when they're obviously female. An alto is a male singer who uses falsetto, rather like a low counter-tenor. What's a contralto? In the old days, when categorising of the human voice was clearer, a contralto could be confirmed if the chest register sounded like a tenor. Hence the manly sound of Dame Clara Butt, Louise Kirkby-Lunn and, more recently, Ewa Podles. Mezzos should have the same vocal range as a soprano – two and a half octaves including a high C – but they prefer to sing lower. This confuses some singers and gives them a false start. A couple of well-known mezzos have had quite good careers early on as 'light mezzos', when they are actually lazy sopranos. That is, sopranos who never take the time to extend their technique to encompass the higher register but sing comfortably in the lower regions, without the ringing chest notes required by mezzos.

Mezzos can be placed in various repertoire categories. There's the trouser role type, the glamour mezzo (these roles are few and far between), the mezzo who sings roles originally written for castrati, the Rossini mezzo (or contralto) roles and the older character mezzo, not to mention the commonplace mezzo roles as maids, bitches and best friends. Even earlier than that is the 'boy' role. Cecilia Bartoli made her debut still in her single-figure years singing the offstage shepherd in Puccini's *Tosca*. The great Giulietta Simionato sang the same role on the historic studio recording from 1938 which starred Beniamino Gigli and Maria Caniglia, though she was a little older than Bartoli.

Usually, when a mezzo is young she is cast in what are known as trouser roles, playing parts that require her to wear boys' costumes on stage. The most obvious of these are Mozart's Cherubino (the rather lovable naughty boy in *The Marriage of Figaro*) and Sesto in *La Clemenza di Tito*. Over a century later, Richard Strauss created two wonderful, slightly more mature, characters, the title role of Octavian in *Der Rosenkavalier* and the Composer (that's his only name and he appears only in the prologue) in *Ariadne auf Naxos*. There is a physical requirement for all these roles: small hips and no boobs. Singers playing Cherubino frequently have to wear an undergarment that flattens the chest. Some are clever with the disguise, others less so.

Whereas Mozart's Sesto is very much a 'stand and sing' character, his Cherubino is a big part of the action, darting around the stage creating mischief and avoiding discovery. Petite sopranos sometimes steal this role from their lower-voiced sisters. In fact some famous sopranos of the past have alternated Cherubino with Cio Cio San in *Madama Butterfly*. I suppose both roles are physically diminutive but big on personality. The Strauss roles are, perhaps, more modern theatrically. The Composer is a complex young man deciding whether his work (that is, the opera he's written) is going to achieve success. Octavian is a truer portrait of a young man in love. The opening scene of this very glamorous opera finds him and the Marschallin (Princess von Werdenberg) in bed together. I remember a school friend returning from a performance of this opera wondering why there were two women on stage making out!

The French like their transvesti roles too. Charles Gounod crafted two splendid boy roles for mezzo – Siebel in *Faust* and Stephano in *Roméo et Juliette*. Both are perky boys, deeply in love with the opera's heroine. In both cases, the object of their affection dies in the final scene. In Jacques Offenbach's *Les Contes d'Hoffmann*, the mezzo dressed as a boy Nicklausse also doubles as the Muse with two strings to his bow. Nicklausse gets to start the famous Barcarolle duet with Giulietta, which opens the Venetian scene.

In the 17th and 18th centuries, before the advent of the star tenor or soprano, the famous opera celebrities were definitely the castrati. Funnily enough, these vocal types no longer exist. For those of you who are unaware of the details, a boy's manhood was tampered with some years before puberty so that his singing voice would remain high. (I presume that it was even higher during the operation.) There are many ways this procedure was done – all disturbing – but the 'kindest' was to make the child soak in a hot bath until his entire body was soft and prune-like. The medical practitioner would then squeeze his testicles until they were destroyed. This would preserve the soprano quality of the voice while the boy's body grew in size. With that physical growth came the strengthening of the muscles. After studying castrato singing for seven years, these boys would emerge with extraordinary vocal techniques and giant bodies. This growth occurred because the testosterone levels could not be directed to the natural places on the body, so they were tall, slightly effeminate, fabulous singers with loud voices. They could perform any vocal trick required. Huge vocal ranges, enormous breath capacity, vocal dexterity – they had it all in abundance and the world swooned at their feet. They were the rock stars of their day. Several were even reported to have had affairs with their female fans. At least it was safe sex. The age of castrati came to an end in the mid-nineteeth century.

The composers of the day knew that their own celebrity would be assured if the castrati sang their music and a huge number of major roles were written for this breed. Handel and Hasse were renowned for their castrati operas and their vocal writing was tailored to the needs of these great technicians. In modern times, the roles written for castrati are now contracted to either counter-tenors (who, on most occasions, give a limp reading of something that was meant to be powerful) or to handsome mezzos in trousers. Joan Sutherland, who was partly responsible for the Handel revival in the late 1950s, told me that she'd rather have a good mezzo any day singing opposite her than a counter-tenor. Joan had her fair share of good, handsome mezzo colleagues during her career. Her most famous partnership was with the American Marilyn Horne. Their vocal qualities perfectly blended like a good hot chocolate and their onstage duets were legendary. Sutherland had great moments with other mezzos – Huguette Tourangeau, Monica Sinclair and Margreta Elkins

– but the combination of Joan and Jackie (Horne's pet name) surpassed all others.

It was Marilyn Horne who showed her true mettle at London's Royal Opera House during a performance of Rossini's *La Donna del Lago*. Some noisy patrons were seated in one of the high loges – the boxes at the side of the stage where the really budget-priced seats are located. Whether they were paid to disrupt the show by claques or they were just fans of a rival mezzo, they booed loudly at the end of Horne's big solo scene. Horne, who by this time had been a major singer for several decades, took note of the location of the offending patrons. At her final curtain call they again started to boo, this time louder than before. Horne, dressed in a kilt, sporran and feathered cap (because it's a Scottish opera) waved her arms to silence the audience. When you could hear a pin drop, Horne coldly looked up at the loge, pulled up her sleeves, clenched her fists and called out in her clearest American accent, 'I know who you are. Come down here and I'll fix you!' The normally subdued British audience went wild. It's memories like these that remind you how wonderful the theatre can be.

Gioacchino Rossini wrote his operas during the last days of the castrati. Indeed, his great 1810 opera, *Tancredi,* has a castrato in the title role. It seems incredible that Rossini wrote many roles for the mezzo voice rather than the soprano sound. This could have been spurred on by his marriage to

Isabella Colbran who was a very great contralto. Several of the roles were designed specifically for her voice and lay in the lower reaches of the mezzo register. When you hear the comic roles of Rosina in *Il Barbiere di Siviglia*, Angelina in *La Cenerentola* or Isabella in *L'Italiana in Algeri* sung by a fruity mezzo, the character jumps out at you. When you have a mezzo Semiramide singing with a contralto Arsace in *Semiramide* it sounds just right. Arsace, who turns out to be Semiramide's son, and Isolier in *Le Comte Ory* are Rossini's most prized trouser roles.

Whether they didn't have access to a soprano or they felt sorry for the plight of the mezzo we'll never know, but Dalila in Camille Saint-Saëns' *Samson et Dalila*, Bizet's Carmen, Charlotte in Massenet's *Werther*, Ambroise Thomas' Mignon, Dido in Berlioz's *Les Troyens* and Leonore di Gusman in Donizetti's *La Favorite* are principally glamour roles for the mezzo voice. Of course, we constantly see and hear sopranos invading this territory but it really is the mezzo's domain. Each of these women forms the central interest to the opera's plot. With the exception of Mignon, they are sexy creatures with big personalities. Their solo music is rather gorgeous too. Dalila has three drop-dead arias, Charlotte has two, Mignon is an old-fashioned girl with three arias, Leonore di Gusman has a great scene that she sometimes sings in the original French and *Carmen* is riddled with magnificent pages for the protagonist. Berlioz's

Dido is a profound and lovely character with pages of gorgeous music.

There are a few quirky roles beloved by mezzos. The bearded lady Baba the Turk in Igor Stravinsky's *The Rake's Progress* is a tour de force for an intelligent actor singer. I use the word intelligent because, without the use of the brain in this repertoire, many angry words can be thrown around the rehearsal room. The music is tricky, not too melodious and the performer needs to have a flair for comedy. Thirty years later, Stephen Sondheim's Mrs Lovett in *Sweeney Todd* demands the same skills of a character mezzo, but without the beard.

If you want to venture into the French operettas of Offenbach, it takes a real celebrity mezzo to bring off the title roles in *La Périchole*, *La Grande-Duchesse de Gérolstein* and *La Belle Hélène* with suitable aplomb. In the Italian literature the Verdi roles of Amneris in *Aida* and Azucena in *Il Trovatore* are prized accomplishments on the curriculum vitae. They are roles requiring great drama and a lot of gesticulation. It is generally known that Verdi originally contemplated calling the opera *Azucena*. On the subject of opera titles, Grace Bumbry, one of the great mezzos, who moved to the soprano tessitura for nearly two decades, was performing the role of Amneris alongside the Aida of Leontyne Price at the Metropolitan Opera in New York. The applause following Amneris's big solo moment – the judgement scene – was long and loud. Feeling good, Bumbry walked into the wings and, as she passed Price, she said, 'Honey, I don't know why Verdi didn't call this opera *Amneris*'. Leontyne Price brushed her aside and said, 'I'll show you why', and went onstage to sing the glorious tomb scene. She was right. No matter how great the mezzo is performing Amneris, Verdi has provided material of another world for Aida.

One of the most famous theatrical moments for a soprano and mezzo is the scene that closes Act One of Donizetti's *Maria Stuarda*. Although historically incorrect – Elizabeth I and Mary Queen of Scots never met face to face – Donizetti's story climaxes when Elizabeth confronts Mary and publicly taunts her rival until breaking point. Mary ends up denouncing Elizabeth with a savage aria that begins 'Figlia impura di Bolena' (Impure daughter of Bolena, i.e. Anne Boleyn) and ends with 'Vil bastarda al tuo pie' (Vile bastard at your feet). It's great stuff and fabulous when everyone is on fire.

Some artists are born to serve others. Artists on a company's weekly salary may be scheduled to perform the non-glamorous roles of maids and friends. Sometimes they are memorable cameos. Who was it who said, 'There are no small roles, only small players'? Character mezzos can also make great impressions on the public. Violetta's maid Annina and her friend Flora in *La Traviata* are good parts though not substantially long in duration.

Desdemona sings a desperate 'addio' to her maid Emilia in Verdi's *Otello*, Gilda confides in Giovanna in *Rigoletto*, Marguerite is under the thumb of Martha in *Faust*, Mallika gets to sing one of the most famous duets in all opera with her mistress Lakmé, little Lucia di Lammermoor seems to always hang around Alisa and a good Suzuki (the biggest maid role of them all) can make Butterfly seem even more tragic. Puccini's other maid role, the Indian squaw Wowkle in *La Fanciulla del West* (*The Girl of the Golden West*) merely grunts her few lines in Act Two. Petra in Sondheim's *A Little Night Music* gets only a few brief phrases to sing before her 11 o'clock number 'The Miller's Son'. That's one of opera's strangest star spots.

It seems more appealing to be someone's friend in opera. That way you get better things to sing. Norma's friend Adalgisa has three duets and a nice aria to display her character. Vanessa, in Samuel Barber's opera of the same name, is sympathetically partnered by her friend Erica. Her aria 'Must the winter come so soon?' is one of the opera's loveliest moments.

In some cases a mezzo can extend her performing career by moving to the older characters of opera, which require a lower voice. There is a multitude of small roles that can only be performed successfully by artists of vast experience. They enhance the works in which they feature but their individual performances do not ensure or destroy the opera's success.

Then there are mezzo roles that do charge a scene with energy when they appear but they're not necessarily on stage for long. Ulrica, the fortune-telling gypsy in Verdi's *Un Ballo in Maschera*, commands the plot – in fact she predicts the end of the opera. Herodias in Richard Strauss's *Salome* and Klytemnestra in his *Elektra* demand the resources of a theatrical mezzo to portray these frightening women. The 'bitch factor' is required. Of course the mother of all bitches is *Lohengrin*'s Ortrud. The vitriol she projects at Elsa and the assembled chorus must to be scary. (Some stage managers do great imitations of Ortrud at parties. Just ask them.)

I've missed out a few well-loved mezzo roles. Mistress Quickly in Verdi's *Falstaff* has the audience on side at all times while the Kostelnicka in Janacek's *Jenufa* is a vehicle for a powerhouse performer. She, like Klytemnestra, Herodias, Amneris and Azucena, should nearly eat the scenery when on stage. It's a theatrical style that is no longer in fashion, but the dramatic music tells you that it must be performed this way. Just as Wagner's Mother Earth Erda, in the early pages of *The Ring,* remains motionless – as does her music – while she sings, the dramatic mezzo roles conceived by Janacek, Strauss and Verdi demand the theatrics of the over-the-top school.

Soon after I began my professional career I worked with a mezzo who had been the first Cherubino I'd seen on stage. She was a laugh-a-minute artist and we certainly never managed to look at each other without smiling. She had a profound vocal gear change between registers which she used as part of her characterisation. I was surprised to learn that she had been a high lyric soprano with Gilda in *Rigoletto* and Adina in Donizetti's *L'Elisir d'Amore* to her credit. An old maestro had advised her, 'If you want to have a long career, learn to be a mezzo.' She followed that advice and forsook young girls in favour of young boys. Her career lasted well after her singing voice had sadly left her, yet she was beloved by the audience.

CARMEN

HISTORY HAS IT that Georges Bizet's *Carmen* was a disaster at its premiere. And, although it is now regarded as one of the most popular operas, it has suffered notorious disasters over the years. Tragically, Bizet died exactly three months after the premiere at the ripe old age of 37. He had been suffering from rheumatism, heart trouble and chronic throat infections, and then came a double heart attack along with a stroke. Perhaps there's been a jinx on this opera from the beginning? Nevertheless, an old source suggests that Célestine Galli-Marié, the creator of the role, saw Bizet's ghost during the Act Three card scene. Whether this is true or not, it's a good story.

As with many other admirers of this opera, my introduction to *Carmen* was via the 78rpm set recorded by that tasteful and classy group of musicians Spike Jones and His City Slickers. To this day, every time I conduct, play or hear the opening chorus 'Sur la place, chacun passe, chacun vient, chacun va', I can't not hear 'We're the girls, yes, we're the girls that make the best bubblegum', sung in delectable fashion in my head. Is this crazy? Yes. But it was Spike's version that got me hooked on this great opera. It took me only a matter of days to realise that Carmen didn't actually have eyes of different colours or that what she really liked to do was 'roll the bone'. (I never found out what that was – probably best not to know.)

Carmen has four acts, four main characters (although in the old days Escamillo and Micaela were classed as small roles), four smaller roles and a handful of male roles of even lesser importance. There's a grand story that rapidly runs from nice to nasty. The story opens on the hottest and most boring day known in Seville. The guards and soldiers are occupying their time playing cards and smoking while a group of child choristers perform a small version of their own military routine. (Producers like to have children in a production because they bring along their sisters, their cousins and their aunts –hence more ticket sales.) Morales, corporal of the guard, and his Lieutenant Zuniga fill in time sorting out the marching male chorus. Just before that, a homely looking young girl in the plainest costume in the history of operatic costume design enters and asks to speak with Don José. Another corporal of the guard, Don José is the principal tenor. Because the soldiers have been away from the feminine kind for so long, they tease Micaela in a way that is currently inappropriate in the workplace and she goes out feeling a little ruffled. The lunchtime bell rings and the soldiers sing about looking forward to seeing the working girls from the cigarette factory coming out for siesta. They appear each holding a lighted cigarette and attempting to outdo each other in the sexy acting stakes. In actual fact, this group looks more like the rejects from Miss Spain 1940. No sooner are they assembled on stage than we hear the 'fate' motif. It is first heard in a fast tempo and the men sing something to the effect that Carmencita is about to make her entrance. She does and she sings the famous Habanera.

This tremendously well-known aria is in the staple repertoire diet of almost every mezzo soprano. Sopranos also perform the title role – and I sometimes prefer this higher voice type over the lower, fruitier mezzo. It is a little-known fact that Bizet stole the tune of the Habanera from an old song, 'El Arreglito', by Yradier. Bizet wasn't the first to pilfer a good tune. What's a little sequence of notes among friends? The jist of this Habanera is to inform everyone that Carmen is free with her love but 'If you love me, take care'. You'd think that they'd already guess it from her sexy stage demeanour. Anyway, there's one guy on stage who seems not to notice her and, as we know from our past relationships, that can upset a girl. Carmen goes over to Don José and gives him a flower. This turns into an act of ridicule but the tenor remains oblivious as Carmen's entourage vacates the stage.

I have very clear memories of this moment at one matinée performance. The mezzo soprano, a Polish woman with an eccentric personality, was one of those who believed that, to get into the character, it was necessary not to wear knickers under her costume. (Stagehands don't seem to mind this practice.) For some strange reason a whole stream of famous and not-so-famous Carmens have followed the no-knickers tradition. It is beyond me what it could bring to the role! Our Polish mezzo would improvise at will, which could unnerve the other performers. At her exit from this scene, the stage director had asked her to take a last-minute glance at the chorus, then quickly disappear through a doorway. It was a nice concept ahd she did it effectively. Matinée performances are frequently attended principally by an aged audience who don't like going out at night. They like to see 'nice' things on stage like in the 'old days'. At this matinée, our Carmen, minus panties, and really in character, did everything as usual except at the exit. Sure enough, she gave Don José the flower, but when she went to go through the doorway, she turned and looked at everyone in the theatre and said, in a loud clear voice, 'Get f—-ed!' (Actually her thick accent left off the 'd'.) This was a slight deviation from scripted dialogue but she also seemed to forget that the sung lyrics and spoken dialogue – except for this – were in the original French. Had I been able to see the faces of the audience (the ones who could hear) I'd imagine that they'd have resembled those fortunate to enjoy Mel Brooks' 'Springtime for Hitler'. Needless to say, her unusual behaviour was noted by management and she never got the opportunity to perform the role again – with or without her panties.

Micaela appears with a letter from Don José's mother. Micaela secretly loves Don José and, if he returned the affection, we'd have no story. In the original Prosper Mérimée novel, the character of Micaela does not even appear. One can only assume that she was added by the librettists Ludovic Halévy and Henri Meilhac to build family interest. Together the tenor and soprano sing an emotional, lyrical duet filled with memories for both characters. Now the rot sets in. A scream is heard offstage. It's one of the cigarette girls alerting everyone that a fight has broken out in the factory. Sure enough, Carmen is to blame. Zuniga arrests her and, depending on the production, Don José is instructed to handcuff Carmen or bind her wrists with rope. Sure enough, they are left alone and Carmen seduces her captor into freeing her wrists and escaping together to a café on the corner. She does this while singing the famous Seguidilla.

By the time we get to Act Two, we are already at Lillas Pastia's inn and there's an exotic dance happening. Carmen has made friends with Frasquita and Mercedes and they join in the celebrations. An offstage chorus is heard announcing the arrival of the famous toreador

Escamillo and as soon as they sing the repeat of the jaunty chorus he arrives, just in time to sing his hit tune. We've already heard it in the middle of the orchestral prelude (the short overture) but, of course, his performance is much better. The aria is exploding with testosterone – so much so, that the choristers join in. Following the huge ovation from the audience, there's some small talk with Carmen and he leaves with the full adulation of the chorus. Now the story really gets going.

Soon two rugged-looking guys appear and we soon discover that they are smugglers – smugglers who manage to sing a really musically tricky quintet. (Oscar Hammerstein II wrote some splendid updated lyrics for this ensemble in his *Carmen Jones*.) Carmen, Frasquita, Mercedes, Remendado and Dancairo sing about their illegal plans to make money. In the middle, Carmen astounds everyone by announcing that she's in love. No sooner is this revealed than we hear another offstage voice. It's Don José singing a song from his dragoon days. Carmen prepares a nice picnic spread and tries to turn him on. This can't be happening – he's got an aria to sing in a few bars and he has to concentrate. They have a small tiff and he reaches into his costume and presents the flower that she gave him in Act One. Amazingly it's still as fresh as the day it was picked even though it has been pressed to his heart underneath his coat for weeks. (That's the glory of fake flowers.) His aria happens and it's all about the flower and his love for Carmen. She encourages him to run away to the hills to join the band of smugglers. Like the puppy that he is, Don José agrees. Another offstage voice is heard, this time Lieutenant Zuniga, who's come to enjoy a lap-dance from Carmen. Don José confronts him and, before we know it, Zuniga is taken prisoner and the stage is filled with everyone, except Escamillo, singing that the hills are soon to be alive with the sound of their music.

We find out, quick smart, in Act Three that life as a smuggler is not all it's cracked up to be. Usually the costumes are not flattering, the stage lighting is dark, and the only redeeming feature in the scene is Bizet's music. With the chorus asleep and Remendado and Dancairo keeping watch, the three girls get down to playing card games. This is fortune telling at its scariest. Frasquita and Mercedes shuffle the deck and produce the cards that confirm that there will be fortune and happiness ahead for both. Not to be outdone, Carmen takes hold of the pack and the first card to reveal itself is diamonds immediately followed by spades. This signals only one thing – *death*! (Why couldn't it be hearts? Well, we need an Act Four.) As she sings of her cruel destiny, enhanced by the repetition of the fate motif, the other two girls vocally laugh with the thrill of their good fortune. Musically and theatrically it's one of those great moments in opera. Tragically, the first production of *Carmen* I saw featured a very large woman who seemed to have a cat sitting on her head – it was, in fact, a very bad wig – and her acting of this scene was ghastly. Joining that memory was the matching cat-on-head wig worn by the Escamillo who was her real-life husband. Even though the opera was sung in an English translation, I couldn't understand a word. Again, Bizet was clearly the winner.

The first time I conducted a *Carmen* season of my own, I had the good fortune to have a fabulously sexy Swedish mezzo in the title role. She was a great colleague and an honest actor, with a very naughty sense of humour. After one performance I mentioned that her positioning at her initial entrance – high on a set of stairs – and her physical contortions on those stairs during the Habanera gave me a direct view up her skirt. I thought that was shocking enough but her reaction of 'Could you see my knickers?' rather shocked one of the sponsors attending the supper. During the rehearsal period of that production I made playing cards of my own. One card had a childish drawing of a carrot, the other an equally innocent-looking pig. I replaced the prop cards with these so that on Carmen's 'Carreau' (meaning diamonds) she turned over the carrot card – so too with the Pig for 'Pique' (spades). It lightened a rather heavy afternoon's work. When we came to that same place in the score on the final performance of the season, she turned the first card and declaimed 'Carreau', then finished the word with a very clear 't'. Sure enough, she looked straight at me on the podium and sang 'Pig' for her next phrase. There must have been a handful of people in the audience who wondered what the hell she was doing, but her naughtiness made me love her more.

There's an uplifting ensemble where everybody gets a go at a solo but, in theatrical terms, it's there merely to get the stage cleared for the arrival, after about an hour and half, of Micaela. She's searched out the smugglers' lair and asks God to give her confidence to face this terrible mezzo who has distracted Don José. She also prays for legato and a good top B. After a few curtain calls, there's a gunshot offstage – and she hides behind a part of the scenery. Who's there? Escamillo has stumbled into Carmen's hiding place and he's caught by Don José. This is one of the few times that Don José catches anything. There are some confrontational macho stances, followed by a struggle but they both cease when restrained by members of the chorus. Carmen's eyes flash with the memory of how attracted she is to the toreador and Escamillo tips his hat and departs. Remendado notices a bush trying to hide Micaela. She's dragged out to centre stage and belittled when Carmen realises her identity. She pleads with Don José to return to his mother, who's now at death's door. This is a wonderful time for the tenor to show off his lung capacity. Torn between Mother and Micaela, he rants and raves, culminating in a sustained high A. Just before the curtain comes down we hear the voice of Escamillo in the refrain of his song. That's just in case we'd forgotten...

I should have mentioned earlier that Bizet wrote orchestral preludes to each act. The first one we hear contains the very famous Toreador tune along with the energetic chorus theme. The second quotes the dragoon ditty that Don José sings as he enters the scene of the flower aria. Act Three is preceded by a moving flute solo accompanied by a harp. It grows as the other woodwind instruments join in counterpoint. For the Act Four prelude, Bizet composed a fabulous Spanish dance that is typically French in style.

There's pandemonium as Act Four opens. We have programme sellers, orange sellers, townsfolk and a noisy children's chorus all competing to be the loudest as they jump for joy that Escamillo is in town. Yes, we hear 'that tune' a few times more. He's here and with Carmen, looking great in a flash costume, on his arm. They sing their 25 bars of duet as he enters the stadium to face the bull. Then follows a short moment where Frasquita and Mercedes warn Carmen to 'take care'. That's an understatement. They also leave the scene.

The stage is left bare, except for Carmen. Then Don José, looking the worse for wear, staggers on. There's a lot of big-eye acting from José and some snarling from Carmen. For once in her life she allows fate to take its course and dares Don José to kill her – and he does. It takes a few more minutes and some pretty dramatic singing from both of them. Might I add that, wedged between each musical accusation from the pair onstage, is an offstage chorus updating us on the progress of the bull fight.

It never ceases to amaze me how much performers ask of the imagination of the audience. That first *Carmen* I attended had the Don José stabbing Carmen as if he were mashing a sack of potatoes. The Polish mezzo mentioned earlier was unable to die as planned because her mantilla got caught on the wall of the set and it was so well attached to her wig – and her wig firmly glued to her head – that she died standing. I've had to rehearse Carmens who, in a split second, have to find a small mark on the wall that will ooze the blood supposedly from her back as the bullet (the director's weapon of choice in this production) goes through her. That was an idea that, for me, made sense. One well-respected but temperamental tenor, who was performing Don José on tour in Chicago, had obviously fallen out with the leading lady. During the final scene he dropped his knife, shouting, 'Finish it yourself!' and Carmen had to stab herself to death.

LA FORZA DEL DESTINO

ANY MENTION OF this opera always brings back memories of the early years of my career when I acted as prompt for several seasons of *La Forza del Destino*. Because I was new to the business, and a bit of a clown, several pranks were played on me by colleagues. The prompt box was only accessible via the stage and a stage manager had to push the curtain over the box to enable my exit. I must have been particularly rude to staff one night and they 'forgot' to attend to my exit. I had to stay in the cramped box suspended over the orchestra pit throughout the entire interval! Another time, in a theatre that had a temporary prompt box placed in the orchestra pit, I had to enter with the band and climb in before the performance started. My head was seen by the stage but I couldn't see anything below me in the cramped space except for the vocal score. During the performance I felt something being bound around my ankles. It wasn't until the conclusion of the show that I was able to see that tape had secured my feet and I was unable to move. I think there was a lot of shouting later that day. On another occasion, again during a season of this magnificent opera, I made the prompt box just in time before the start of the show. Little did I know that someone had discovered my phobia for birds' feathers. Need I say more? The final performance of that particular run was fun for the whole chorus but not for me. As they exited in line, each – in time to the music – threw the contents of their food bowls over me in the box. The remaining minutes of the opera were supported by a drenched and sticky prompt.

Verdi's opera, written for St Petersburg in 1862, is an amazing piece of theatre. The musical surge of the score sweeps the audience with an urgency not experienced in many other works. It's actually the music that holds the rather ridiculous story together and allows the audience to have some semblance of reality. Some operas take you to the brink. Teetering on the edge is *La Forza del Destino*.

When you buy a ticket for a production of this work, you can never be sure what version – or how much of it – you'll be seeing. The original St Petersburg version plays for several hours and has an unexpected bit of drama at the end. As he did with several of his other operas, Verdi revised *La Forza del Destino* for his native Italian audiences. It's this newer version that is most often performed.

The choice of version isn't the only decision that has to be made with this opera. The order of the scenes and placement of the overture are also points of contention. Traditionally, many theatres have placed the overture between Acts One and Two. This is a crafty way of saving scene-change time. It's a lengthy show and the longer the orchestra, chorus and stage crew are working, the more expensive it becomes. The playing time for the overture is about eight minutes, which is just enough time to move one bit of scenery off the stage and a new bit on, all with the curtain down. I have been personally reprimanded for this placement by press critics who have read academic books and are concerned that the structure is wrong. Verdi titled this great bit of orchestral writing 'Sinfonia', which is quite different from an overture. The latter should be placed at the beginning as it introduces the flavour, drama and tunes. A sinfonia is just a good bit of music you can play anywhere.

Act One begins with some low bassoon chords. From these you can almost sense the foreboding. We're in a room in the Calatrava Castle and the Marchese di Calatrava is bidding his 'Buona nottes' (nighty-nights) to his daughter Donna Leonora di Vargas. In the corner is the maid Curra. Can you guess that she's a mezzo soprano? You can guess that we're in Spain – the location for so many good operatic stories – by the costumes and the fact that almost every character's name begins with 'Don'. From an early age, Leonora (for short) has been a moody girl and this night is no different. She is almost monosyllabic when answering her father. He goes off and Curra mumbles that everything is ready as planned. In a rather divine aria, Leonora lets us in on what she's been thinking about for days. She's racked with guilt and terrified at the prospect of her future in a strange land – she's been seeing Don Alvaro (a dramatic tenor) and they plan to elope this very night. No sooner does she greet the applause for her rendition of the aria 'Me pellegrina ed orfana' (A wanderer and orphan) than Alvaro runs in, full of energy. His music is heroic, youthful and full of passion. This is where the lighting designer has been directed to dim the lights to almost pitch darkness. The sort of tenor capable of singing the role of Alvaro very rarely looks 'heroic, youthful and full of passion'. Usually, he's wearing contact lenses the thickness of coke bottles and he's vertically challenged. (This is the first instance in the performance where the audience is asked to forget reality.) Because he and Leonora haven't seen each other since wishing each other good luck in their dressing rooms, they sing a duet about how happy they're going to be once they escape the dreary confines of the Calatrava mansion.

At the musical climax of the fast ending to the duet, the Marchese comes back having heard noise that sounds something like applause. He's been wary that there was trouble afoot and he's not wrong. He denounces Don Alvaro for seducing his daughter. To proclaim his innocence, Alvaro takes out his gun to surrender and what happens? It accidentally fires a bullet into the Marchese. Looking up from the podium at this point is entertaining and you always seem to be shaking your head as you look down at the next page in the score. With great actors the scene would play like this: The tenor takes out the gun. It fires. The bass jolts his body to suggest the bullet shock. He gasps and falls to the ground. This should take place in a matter of four musical bars (and they're fast). Generally the sequence of this scene occurs in no particular order. I've seen the bass shot before the gun goes off. Everyone has noted the gun not firing at all in at least one of their *La Forza del Destino* outings. There's a tale of Enrico Caruso, the greatest tenor ever, in the early years of the 20th century, forgetting to bring on the pistol and holding up his finger and shouting, 'Bang!!' Some theatres cannot legally allow singers – or even actors – to fire their own prop guns so a stage manager attempts to synchronise the sound offstage. Need I tell you that this *never* works? Anyway, the bass playing the Marchese di Calatrava curses Leonora and quickly dies as Alvaro and Leonora run off into the night. This is not a good way to leave your home. The curtain rapidly comes down as the sinfonia (or overture) is played.

Act Two is where things start getting messy. We now find ourselves at an inn in the village of Hornachuelos. All the locals are drinking and they are joined by a mysterious character disguised as a student. There's nothing unusual about students partaking of liquor but this one really is Don Carlo di Calatrava, the brother of Leonora and son of the dead Marchese di Calatrava. He's also, obviously, a mature student. For a brief moment we see Leonora enter the inn, dressed in men's clothing. Looking around, she recognises her disguised brother and flees to a room upstairs. (The librettist has failed to let us know that, in the night-time elopement, Leonora and Alvaro became separated and each now assumes the other is dead. It's a very logical assumption ...)

With a celebrity entrance, we are introduced to a mezzo soprano who isn't a maid or a woman dressed as a boy. Her name is Preziosilla and she's a gypsy drumming up recruits for the war. In a rather flamboyant aria, she urges all the boys to head for Italy and fight the Germans. This is followed by a Preighiera (prayer) started by some pilgrims who've wandered into the picture. (When you want a prayer, throw some nuns, priests, monks – anything remotely religious – onstage.) It's a nice, still moment where all the vocal sections onstage get to be noticed – all supporting the descant of Leonora who has come out of her room unnoticed by everyone except the audience. She prays that God will save her from her brother's vengeance.

As Preziosilla has gypsy powers she is not fooled by Don Carlo's disguise. She reads his hand and states that he's not who he claims to be, then exits. The scene now changes to the entrance of a monastery of the Madonna degli Angeli. It's supported by music reminding us of Leonora's anxious state of mind. She comes looking for a safe haven, singing a great recitative and aria, supported by an offstage chorus of monks. She prays for the forgiveness of her soul and the fact that her legs look ridiculous in these pants.

One favoured old school diva was rehearsing Leonora, her 'calling card' role. During this magnificent scene she was walking grandly around the stage in her trouser costume making the grandest of gestures. The stage director had been waiting for the best moment to give her this difficult note on her characterisation. 'Darling, you're moving around the stage like a diva would. Leonora is not a diva.' She thought for a second and we heard her response, given with a twinkle in her eye: 'Oh yes she is!' The same soprano was later heard saying to the director, with some frustration, 'Honey, let me just do it and I'll put the moves in later.'

Ringing a bell and chatting with a very unfunny comic character called Fra Melitone, who is always wigged and costumed to look like Friar Tuck, Donna Leonora finally meets the head honcho of the monastery, Padre Guardiano. He's a fatherly bass of the sympathetic variety, in a role that demands exceptional artistry. The first time I conducted the opera I was lucky to convince a much-respected American bass, Joshua Hecht, to leave the safety of his retirement and perform Padre Guardiano again, a role he had first performed almost 50 years before. As he was a protégé of the great American soprano Rosa Ponselle who had debuted in the role of Leonora with Caruso and was universally accepted as his vocal equal, I felt that lineage had been passed through him to me. Need I say that his performance was one of the greatest experiences of my career? His vocal ease, his theatrical expertise and his terrible jokes made him the star of the production. He even made his own stage beard. We thought he did this so he'd look like the Almighty Himself.

Getting back to the story. Leonora surprises Guardiano by revealing that she's actually a woman. Some of the Leonoras I've seen would make even Helen Keller question Guardiano's reaction. She goes on and on about the story we've just experienced and pleads for sanctuary. He agrees that a life of penance and solitude would be good to atone her sins as well as help her lose weight. He arranges for her to live in a remote cave with only a bell to summon help. Without thinking, she agrees. The scene shifts to the moment of sacrament. Padre Guardiano warns of a curse on anyone who violates the sanctity of the cave or discloses its inhabitant's identity and Act Two concludes with a ravishing scene where Leonora sings of her devotion to the namesake of the monastery. This is where we have interval drinks – or, in my case, go round to tell the soprano how fantastically she is singing.

In Act Three we're now in Velletri, Italy, where fighting ensues between the Spanish soldiers and the Austrian invaders. During a pretty clarinet solo we are reintroduced to Don Alvaro. He's not dead at all – in fact, at the end, he's going to be one of the few still standing. He and his best friend, aka Don Carlo(!), have joined the Spanish contingent under false names and are unbeknown to each other. Isn't fate weird?

Don Alvaro bemoans his fate – the shame of his mixed blood (did you know that?) and prison birth and the pain of having both deserted his love and inadvertently killed her father. It's a rather messy situation. He hears a cry of help and runs off to save Don Carlo. They swear eternal friendship. Don Alvaro has to leave and asks Don Carlo to look after a small casket, the contents of which must be burned after his death. Temptation gets the better of Don Carlo and he opens the box to find a portrait of his sister and realises that Don Alvaro is his old enemy. Sure enough, he sings a big aria about it. They meet and agree to fight a duel but are interrupted by a returning patrol. Thinking the better of it, Don Alvaro decides to seek shelter in a monastery. You know that this story is going to get yucky. Preziosilla appears and everyone sings a Rataplan – a spirited march tune – to dispel the gloom that has descended on the troops. It's a good part of the score although I've never known any performer who likes it. It is, for the most part, unaccompanied – 'Acapulco: without any musical accomplishment' as a friend used to say – except for a couple of side-drums. At the very end there's a fabulous brass fanfare as the curtain comes down.

After a brief scene change we are inside the monastery of the Madonna degli Angeli. It's supper time and the poor are being fed by charity. Melitone and Guardiano combine their voices in a duet and then the chorus leaves. A second later we are outside the same monastery and Don Carlo demands to see Don Alvaro, who is now a monk. There's a fabulous duet here that includes some very famous tunes. Alvaro is torn between his mind and his gut instinct. He doesn't want to dishonour Leonora. Eventually the tension breaks and they draw swords. They go off fighting.

Now comes the popular 'Pace, pace, mio Dio' (Peace, grant me peace, O Lord) soprano aria. Leonora appears at the doorstep of her cave. We haven't seen her for about 90 minutes and she's still waiting for the peace that seems to have eluded her. 'Misero pane' (Miserable bread) she sings, looking over at a basket filled with a bit of plastic prop bread. She hears someone coming towards her cave, rushes to get her staff to ward off the intruder but thrills us all with a very loud high B flat as she disappears. The clicking of swords is heard offstage and there's a loud 'Ouch' from Carlo as he's been stabbed. Alvaro rings Leonora's bell, as he used to do, for assistance. She appears. Alvaro recognises her and explains what has happened. Rushing over to Carlo, she gives him his opportunity for revenge and he stabs her as he dies. In the closing scene Leonora dies, but not before she sings about the joy she and Alvaro will have together when they finally meet in heaven. The final words come from Padre Guardiano as be blesses Leonora's soul. I think back to that magnificent bass filling every corner of the theatre with the beauty of his tone, and enveloping me with his 'Salita a Dio!' (She's gone to God).

THE MARRIAGE
OF FIGARO

THERE'S A WONDERFUL story, and I hope it's a true one, of two friends who were trombonists in a professional orchestra that was engaged to play for a season of opera at the local theatre. One of the operas was Mozart's *The Marriage of Figaro,* the other a rather more dramatic piece in the operatic repertoire. Now these friends had been drinking buddies for many years and grabbed every opportunity to partake of a beverage or two, much to their wives' dismay. It is generally known that Mozart was quite particular in selecting what instruments he wanted for his compositions and, in the case of *The Marriage of Figaro,* trombones are not required. It was a perfect opportunity. The trombone buddies could use that free night to visit the local hotel while their spouses assumed that they were in the theatre pit sliding away. All was well until they were informed that their wives had bought tickets to see the Mozart performance that night. The tickets were for seats in the front row centre where the wives would have a great view of the orchestra and could feel proud watching their husbands work. To save face – and their marriages – the men went into the pit, took their places and pretended to play with the orchestra. Can you imagine the conductor's face when he looked up and noticed two extra instruments in his band? In music from the classical period, brass instruments are used only occasionally. It must have been a joy for all to see the brass players energetically faking those fast semiquavers that abound in the overture.

Let me tell you of my first *Figaro* experience. I was just in secondary school and attended what turned out to be the last performance by a well-loved ensemble cast. The artists had carved their own personalities into the roles and it was a believable and memorable reading. Years later I found myself working with all but one of the performers in that cast and I frequently thought back to the impact that they had made on me as a teenager. That first staged *Figaro* I experienced was sung in the old English translation by Edward Dent. It had been embedded in my mind since I worked with two stalwarts of the Sadler's Wells Opera years who remembered a man sitting in the rehearsals still modifying the translation in the 1950s. It was Edward Dent himself, continuing to make the libretto pertinent to modern audiences.

Several years later I coached and played a new 'whizz-bang' production that used a trendy new English translation. We received a memo from management ordering that not a single word was to be changed: singers are notorious for modifying translations to suit themselves. A copy of the memo had been attached to the score when delivered to the guest artists, who prepare the music elsewhere and come to the first ensemble call note and word perfect. Our first day of the production began with a rehearsal where the conductor went through the entire score with the full cast to explain 'his' reading. All went well until we came to a page of recitative in Act Two. Figaro's line read, 'You'll find my pen is stronger than his sword'. Unfortunately, in the copying of the score, a mark had appeared between 'pen' and 'is' and it looked remarkably like a hyphen. Yes, the baritone had learnt the original two words as one – and thought nothing strange about it. This true story still ranks high in dinner table anecdotes.

The overture is a splendid piece of froth that bubbles along in the fashion of almost every Mozart opera introduction. It has tremendous energy and delicacy and puts you in the right mood to participate in the drama ahead. The first scene in Act One whizzes along and we meet Figaro and his bride-to-be Susanna. Figaro is doing a bit of stage business measuring the room while Susanna, in front of the mirror, carries on about how lovely her hat is. As is usual with lovers, neither listens to what the other says. Susanna is worried about the droit de seigneur – the right of the lord of the manor – an old custom whereby the aristocrat gets to bed the servant, in this case Susanna, before her wedding. Strangely enough, neither Figaro nor Susanna likes the idea and they decide that, no matter how attractive the baritone playing Count Almaviva is, they will stop it from happening. After all, love *will* find a way. Figaro leaves the room and we get to meet a less attractive woman, Marcellina, and Don Bartolo. Bartolo is a boring bass. Marcellina is a spinster who dislikes Susanna because she's young and spunky and gets to sing a whole lot more. The feeling is mutual. They sing a bitchy duet in which the young woman is rude to the old.

Cherubino, a mezzo soprano dressed as a boy, rushes in telling of his devotion for the Countess Almaviva. He falls in love with anything in a skirt. 'Is it pain? Is it pleasure that fills me?' he sings. There's a rapping at the door and Count Almaviva and Don Basilio enter. Traditionally, Basilio has warts on his nose. I'm not sure what voice type he is – but he's always played by an annoying tenor. Neither of them likes Figaro and both scheme against him. Cherubino hides on a chair and Figaro, who is back in the room, covers it, and him (her), with a piece of fabric. Of course, the new characters do not notice a huge bulge in the shape of a human body under the cloth and proceed to discuss Cherubino's amorous adventures. During this dialogue – or recitative for those requiring technicalities to be accurate – the Count tries to sit on the chair while Figaro distracts him to other locations on the set. A trio ensues and, in describing a previous incident when Cherubino hid under a similar blanket, Count Almaviva uncovers him in exactly the same situation. In angered surprise Almaviva orders Cherubino to go into his regiment, which gives Figaro a great cue to sing the famous aria 'Non piu andrai' (Say goodbye to your pastime and play, lad). The curtain comes down on Act One.

There's a very different mood when the lights come up on the boudoir of the Countess Almaviva. She's not a happy girl. She's miserable with a husband who no longer loves her, and she's still only in her mid-30s. It seems a far cry from when they met in *Il Barbiere di Siviglia* when it was all go. (For those who already know that this story is the middle of a trilogy, skip to the next paragraph.) Rosina and Lindoro (aka Count Almaviva) met in Rossini's (or Giovanni Paisiello's for the know-it-alls) *Il Barbiere di Siviglia*. Of course, Rossini's masterpiece premiered in 1816, 30 years after Mozart's setting of *The Marriage of Figaro*. The characters there remain the same in Mozart except with a couple of voice changes. Basilio, who was Rosina's singing teacher, has moved up from bass to character tenor. He obviously was a decent teacher because, after several years, she's still going strong. Bartolo is still a boring bass and now hangs around Marcellina (aka Berta, the maid). We find out later in Act Three that they've actually done the dirty deed. Next time you sit through the Rossini, keep this in mind.

Meanwhile, in Act Two, the Countess and Susanna are chatting with Figaro and they contrive a plot to trick and embarrass the Count. Cherubino, who has escaped the military, rushes in and asks for ribbons from the Countess's costume. He presents her with a manuscript of a song he's newly composed (in 1786). Not surprisingly, Susanna gets her guitar out and accompanies Cherubino while he performs this rather perfect composition in the style of W.A. Mozart. I'm always amazed at how perfectly Susanna sight-reads this manuscript and makes the solo guitar sound like a full orchestra. I'm also amazed that the rhythm the soprano uses has little to do with what the conductor beats.

Again noise is heard offstage – it's the Count. Cherubino leaves hastily, jumping out of the window. A secret door to the Countess's bedroom has been locked and the Count jealously questions his wife. Her sheepish response makes him suspect that Cherubino has been fooling around again. With his usual pent-up anger he forces the door open, revealing Susanna standing there. It's a great moment in theatre and Mozart's music perfectly complements the drama at this point, as it does throughout the score. The Count is speechless. Figaro enters in full bluster and all seems well until the gardener Antonio puts a spanner in the works. He was working in the garden under the window and something in the shape of a mezzo soprano fell on him. Figaro lies and says that he was the mezzo soprano and that he hurt his ankle in the fall. To further confuse matters, the troupe of Bartolo, Marcellina and Basilio – along with Don Curzio, a lawyer – come in to cause havoc.

Act Three contains two of the standard arias for soprano and baritone, which are presented endlessly at auditions. Mozart cleverly has them placed far enough apart that you don't realise how many times you've heard them. The act opens with a duet between the Count and Susanna. They arrange a meeting in the garden that night. The Count then overhears Figaro and Susanna rejoicing that the case has already been won which prompts the Count to sing his great aria 'Vedrò, mentr'io sospiro' (Must I forgo my pleasure), in which he swears revenge. After mild applause, a swag of characters come in to join the Count. Figaro, Susanna, Marcellina, Bartolo and Don Curzio are discussing the fact that Marcellina plans to marry Figaro because he owes her duemila pezzi duri (2000 crowns). Without the consent of his parents, Figaro cannot accept, especially as he is a 'stolen' child! His proof is a spatula-shaped birthmark on his right arm. Well, you guessed it; he is no other than the child of Marcellina and Bartolo. Marriage, in this case, would be icky and they decide to sing a sextet about it.

Barbarina, the daughter of the the gardener, comes in, chatting with Cherubino. She offers him access to the girls in the castle, dressing him in girl's clothing to disguise him from the Count. The offer is too good to refuse. The Countess, heavy hearted, comes in to sing her divine recitative and aria, 'E Susanna non vien ... Dove sono i bei momenti' (And Susanna's not here ... Where are the happy moments), in which she remembers the happy times of the Rossini opera. Vast applause ensues.

Susanna and the Countess sing a sweet duet while writing a letter to the Count, supposedly from Susanna, reminding him of tonight's assignation in the garden. This is all getting very confusing. They are going to swap costumes to confuse everyone totally and trick the unfaithful husband. There follows a chorus scene where the villagers offer gifts to the bride-to-be. Among them is Cherubino in drag (that is, in double drag). There's some dancing and the curtain falls on Act Three.

Now we're in the garden. After endless solo arias, some quite nice, the action really gets going in the style of a French comedy. The Countess is disguised as Susanna and vice versa. Count Almaviva starts hitting on Susanna, actually his real wife, then becomes jealous as he sees Figaro chatting up what looks to be the Countess (actually ... well, you know). He confronts Figaro just in time for the Countess to reveal her true identity. With his tail between his legs he asks for forgiveness, singing the most sublime phrase you could imagine. Who could resist a baritone on his knees, singing an exquisite legato line and displaying a fabulous voice? Even not-so-good baritones can make this music sound great, such is the genius of Mozart's writing.

We only have about three more minutes before the final curtain. The Countess accepts his apology and everyone sings how pleased they are to have reached the end of the opera in one piece. After all, it's been going for almost four hours, but hours spent with absolute genius.

THE TENOR

YES, ALMOST EVERYTHING you've heard about this strange breed of singer is true. Of all voice types, this is the one that has captured the attention of the general public – or, at the very least, publicists. We've placed the tenor on a pedestal above the baritone, the bass, the mezzo soprano and even the soprano. Why should this be? Is it because they are the most physically attractive of the voice types? Generally this is not the case. The consensus is that the 'natural' male voice is a lower sound and that the tenor voice is an 'unnatural' instrument. Does this mean that audiences prefer to see unnatural acts on stage?

Several of today's celebrity tenors have never performed in an opera. That fact may surprise some readers. The fact that they sing in a vaguely classical tone should not suggest that they are 'opera singers'. In the opera world, we frown on this type of cross-over performer because it misrepresents the true tenor voice. Such singers look good, they're well groomed, they have great physiques, they're charismatic and they sing with the assistance of microphones. In the opera theatre, it is important to project the voice without the use of body mikes (though sound enhancement is definitely employed in major opera theatres) and a weightier physical apparatus is required. A large percentage of tenors do not look like catwalk models but this does not matter if they communicate with a beauty of sound. When a good-looking tenor comes along, as Franco Corelli did in the 1950s, it is even better!

Today a variety of tenor types have an audience following: the Bravura Rossini tenor, the Narcissistic Mozart tenor, the Stand and Sing Loud tenor, the Artistic tenor and the Versatile Character tenor. The Rossini repertoire is a current audience favourite with the type of tenor who specialises in the bravura or flamboyant vocal display. For many years, tenors sang this especially demanding repertoire in a pleasant, perhaps slightly boring fashion. Twenty years ago the operatic world took a turn for the better and a few outstanding vocal athletes came to Rossini's rescue. They brought the hero back into this heroic vocal writing and audiences couldn't get enough. Not only are they proud of their extraordinary vocal feats, they defy you not to appreciate them. These guys excel in rhythmic precision and some even boast vocal ranges that disregard the law of physics.

The Mozart singer is a thing of vocal beauty. He

nurtures every note to make each phrase like a sequence of sparkling gems. A Mozart specialist is musically expressive without the need of the crowd-pleasing high notes. The Mozart tenor would rarely insult the cognoscenti by programming an encore of 'Nessun dorma', even if he was at the football. Perhaps the Artistic tenor would agree with his Mozartian brother. He is also a handsome fellow with a waistline and neck. He really enjoys the beauty of the French repertoire as well as some operatic roles emanating from the British Isles. His ultimate chalice is the high baritone, no aria, role of Pelléas in Claude Debussy's much worshipped opera *Pelléas et Mélisande*. Currently I'm interested in the rarest of the breed, the Stand and Sing Loud tenor – only because he is fast becoming extinct. Audiences, even producers, now cast sensitively musical performers in all roles. They cast light and young, without any knowledge of what the composer or score demands. Almost gone are the days when you could hear a great Enzo in *La Gioconda* or a really great Otello. Where is the like of Lauritz Melchior today for the Wagner repertoire? We have tenors with Melchior's physical size but without his vocal talents.

In one of my first productions as a rehearsal pianist with a professional opera company I worked on Puccini's *Manon Lescaut*. The celebrity soprano was the production's drawcard, and she was quite splendid but she brought her boyfriend, who had been contracted to perform the role of Des Grieux. Rehearsals went smoothly, I thought, but there was friction between the onstage and offstage lovers. As the drama unfolded, neither spoke to each other – which was difficult for everyone because they have a lot of scenes together. There was enormous tension during these moments at every performance until one matinée late in the run. I was still an enthusiastic youngster and attended many performances sitting in the 'perch' on the side of the stage, where the stage technicians keep their equipment. It is usually a good vantage point to observe the onstage action. In Act Two the lovers have not seen each other for a while. Manon's been living in the lap of luxury with an older wealthy suitor and Des Grieux enters her boudoir just after she sings her famous aria and a brief duet with her brother. Puccini provided an extremely passionate duet reuniting the lovers during which they decide that they can't live without each other. Whether it was Puccini's score or something that happened in the dressing room to which I was not privy, the soprano and tenor made up on stage. I've never heard singing like it. They embraced each other with a fire that all of us who have been married know, and clung together as they moved around the stage. Better still, the tenor started to undress the soprano. Funnily enough, it wasn't in the script. That matinée audience actually woke up at this moment and probably thought, 'They didn't do it that way last time I saw it'. As expected, the stage crew had an even closer view and really enjoyed the show.

I love the influences brought to our community by artists from foreign shores. In recent times, I've had the pleasure of working with several Chinese tenors, a couple of whom have exceptionally brilliant voices. Unfortunately none of them had even the slightest grasp of the English language, nor did they understand that the producers require the performer to have committed their role to memory *before* opening night. Singing Calaf in *Turandot* or Alfredo in *La Traviata* in China – and in a Chinese translation – does not mean that it is easy to change the language to Italian. Sometimes when tenors learn something a certain way, it is impossible to change even the slightest musical detail despite what the director or conductor asks. Asian languages are so different from European sounds and many Asian artists have to learn the sung language 'parrot fashion' without any comprehension of the true meaning of the text. As with singers worldwide, some go to the trouble of studying the text word by word but others simply rely on the translation they have sung in a previous non-Italian production. Sung translations and real/literal translations rarely agree. I've experienced many difficult moments when a director can't understand why a performer isn't responding, only to realise that he or she is working from very different material.

A few years back I conducted a production of

Bellini's *Norma* in New Zealand. Because the handsome Chinese-born tenor had had such success singing Calaf in *Turandot* the previous year, and because his strong, healthy voice was perfectly suited to the role, I cast him as Pollione. He had quite an impressive curriculum vitae, but regrettably, he came to the rehearsals totally unprepared. His knowledge of the role was barely adequate. A few tunes had captured his attention but the rest was still quite unknown to him, and he obviously wasn't a quick learner. Throughout the four weeks in the rehearsal room his eyes were glued to the score, which he continued to carry at all times. When he looked away from it he quickly forgot his part. Every time this occurred he would beam and apologise. After many extra hours of study, he managed to remember his vocal line but not the words. When he attempted to add these he would forget everything. As my frustration reached desperation, I suggested that, to keep the production moving, he should sing 'Ah' for the words he could not remember. How wrong was I?

One night he performed the entire role as a 'vocalise' – all on the single vowel 'Ah'. It sounded glorious from beginning to end but did not win the approval of his onstage colleagues, and the audience was confused. Can you imagine singing a passionate love duet with someone who did not sing words? The oddest thing was that, after the performance, he was gleaming with pride that he'd sung so well. At least the audience got the gist of the story from the surtitles.

One splendid tenor of the short, thick-necked variety delivered many moments of joy during his last few years as a performer. His repertoire had steadily built from small roles to the Verdi 'ball busters'. Never a leading man in looks, for a long time he sang a solid and staid Cavaradossi in *Tosca*. In this role he was always assisted by the famous built-up shoes, which looked as if they had been designed for an episode of *Lost in Space*. They added at least an extra 6 inches to his height, bringing him to about 6 inches below the height of the soprano. While extracting his ringing top notes his face would go purple from the effort. Affectionately known to his colleagues as Kenny, he was a simple man who had a great honesty of character as well as a wonderful voice and technique.

On one famous occasion he was rehearsing Beethoven's *Fidelio*. His character Florestan, a political prisoner, appears only in Act Two and is, for most of the action, chained to the set. At one stage rehearsal, the soprano performing Leonora (disguised as the boy Fidelio) stopped and complained every time Ken made a musical error. After the millionth complaint Ken had had enough. He stood up and hurled some strong words at the soprano and stormed off. Well, he would have stormed off had he not been chained by his ankles to the set.

Ken suffered from what the great Anna Russell described as 'having resonance where his brains ought to be'. Everything in life was of secondary importance to his instrument, the voice. One Monday we were starting a revival of the verismo double-bill of *Cavalleria Rusticana* and *Pagliacci,* with music calls all day. The *Pagliacci* was scheduled for the morning rehearsal and Ken was to perform the role of Canio, the guy who sings the great sob aria 'Vesti la giubba' (On with the motley). We waited for him to join the rest of the cast for the ensemble call with the conductor. We waited longer. He didn't appear. Around lunchtime we received a telephone call to explain his absence. Our tenor had been living about ten hours away but planned to stay nearby during rehearsals. He had driven half the journey the day before and stayed with a family member on the Sunday night. Early Monday morning he put a cassette in the car so he could refresh his upcoming role while driving the next three or four hours to rehearsals. After three or four hours he noticed road signs informing him that he was almost back at his starting point – he'd driven in the wrong direction! He eventually arrived, confused and slightly frazzled, but was a knockout at the performances.

Ronald Dowd, a greatly admired tenor from the 1950s to the 1970s in Britain and Australia, enjoyed a career that included meaty roles like Otello, Lohengrin, Tannhäuser, Radames and Florestan, as well as Benjamin Britten's Peter

Grimes, a role on which he had placed his individual stamp. Towards the end of his performing career he was contracted to sing both Turiddu in *Cavalleria Rusticana* and Canio in *Pagliacci* on the same night, as is sometimes done by a celebrity tenor. The venue for the performances was a former boxing arena that had been remodelled for musical and theatrical use. A young friend of mine was in the chorus and, being a conscientious type, wanted to ask advice of the respected tenor. Before a performance he quietly made his way downstairs to the artists' area. As he neared the dressing rooms he heard loud crashing and banging as well as explicit language the like of which he had never encountered before. He found his way to a room that had 'Mr Dowd' on a card over what had previously been 'Gents'. The noise, by this time was very loud. He knocked and heard a voice mutter, 'Come in'. There he found Ronald Dowd surrounded by upturned chairs, some twisted out of recognition, cubicle doors unhinged, costumes and make-up thrown everywhere, and the tenor himself slumped over, bathed in perspiration. 'Thirty years in the business and I still have to change in the f—-ing men's toilet!'

'Er, Mr Dowd, I've been singing as a baritone but I think I might be a tenor. Can I please sing for you so you can let me know what you think?' the young singer asked. The tenor suggested they meet the following morning at 10 a.m. The next morning, the chorister was greeted at the door by

Dowd. On entering the room he went immediately to a piano and played a top C – two octaves above middle C. 'Sing that for me,' urged the tenor. 'I can't sing that straight off without warming up. It's ten o'clock in the morning and we had a show last night,' my friend replied. 'Well, my boy. you're not a tenor. Goodbye!'

Tenors frequently suffer from paranoia. Many people working in this snake-pit business we call opera are similarly afflicted but, because the demands on tenors are heavier, they tend to feel the strain much more. A whole group of tenors from the new generation convince you and their colleagues to expel huge amounts of energy to get them through their performance. 'I'm not good enough. I can't perform the role. Can you please help me?' It took me many years to realise that, with or without assistance, they will perform anyway. The time wasted on pampering them is better spent elsewhere. Perhaps it could be put to positive use by suggesting they sing accurately or on pitch? This type of tenor stops rehearsals every few minutes to ask what he believes is an intelligent question of either the conductor or director. That way all attention is focused on him. By performance time, cast and crew have been running around him for weeks and are emotionally pooped. Then the tenor goes on stage sparking at every moment while his colleagues run on empty.

Some tenors, like blondes, just want to have fun. They continually send themselves up or put themselves down. They are generally liked by their colleagues because they lighten the atmosphere of the rehearsal, frequently blaming themselves for any mistake. In many cases, these performers are also the best actors.

An elderly mentor of mine prompted a famous *Otello* production in London in the late 1950s. The legendary Otello who recorded the role under Arturo Toscanini, Ramon Vinay, sang the title role and, after singing the weighty 'Otello fu' phrase looked down at the prompt and said, 'I bet you didn't know that Otello was Chinese?' My mentor assures me that it's a true story.

Some tenors seem to have all of life's answers. A local tenor had just auditioned and as part of that process had presented references from notable religious figures. An admired and celebrated tenor of a past generation hearing the audition is alleged to have turned and said, 'We'll have to have the doors widened.' When asked why, his reply was 'So he can get his f—ing wings through the door.' This character was also very critical when another tenor didn't use the preferred 'covered' vocal sound, saying 'He's as open as a dunny door up until B flat.' There was a famous incident when he was rehearsing Don José's 'Flower Song' from *Carmen* and experiencing grief from the conductor. The tenor stopped the rehearsal and said. 'Excuse me, Maestro, do you speak English?' When the conductor replied in the affirmative, he said, 'Well just let me sing the f—ing thing.'

Quite recently, I received a message from a budding heldentenor asking for help to build his understanding of the operatic roles of Robert Wagner. Rather than mentioning that he possibly meant Richard Wagner – otherwise we're talking about the handsome American film actor, and I only know a few of his movies – I had to decline his request. It made me think of the soprano Frances Alda's biography, *Men, Women and Tenors*. The title says it all.

MADAMA
BUTTERFLY

WHAT CAN BE said about *Madama Butterfly* that hasn't already been said? Lots. For me, it's a work that remains ever fresh. Each time I come to work on the score there's something new to discover. The story is wonderful and it's a great role for a soprano who has even the slightest dramatic tendencies. She is absolutely the star and even a bad performance can't kill the genius of Signor Puccini.

Before I sat through a staged performance of *Madama Butterfly*, many of the melodies were familiar to me from recordings of the famous arias and duets. I had to see what the fuss was about so as a child, and with only a plot summary, I listened to a recording without interruption. I lasted the two hours' playing time but was confused about why this was such a lauded work. Mind you, I was terribly young and the only relationship I had had was with my teddy bear. What could I have known of Cio Cio San's emotional predicament, even though it was painted so perfectly in the music?

A beloved and noted Cio Cio San once reminisced about her study with the teacher, and legendary soprano, Lotte Lehmann. After seeing the 14-year-old soprano as Mimi in *La Bohème*, Madame Lehmann sent her a note scribbled on the back of a publicity shot, describing her pleasure in the performance. But she suggested that the girl should 'go out and experience life' before singing the role again. The following season, Madame Lehmann attended the same young soprano's first *Madama Butterfly* – yes, she was 15, the actual age of Cio Cio San – and sent another note on the reverse of a photo complimenting her on her quick study of life.

Puccini had been inspired to write the opera after seeing it as a play in the United States. Even though he spoke little English – the language of the play by David Belasco and John Luther Long – he was so moved by the performance that he had to place his operatic stamp on it. Several years later the opera was premiered in Milan but not well received. Puccini revised bits of the score and this version premiered three months later, on 28 May 1904, in Brescia. This is the score that we generally use in performance, though there are sections of Puccini's original that I adore. For instance, the rather small role of Kate Pinkerton is somewhat bigger, more important and extra bitchy. Puccini's later revisions of the opera leave Kate's character fairly faceless. It's a thankless role for the singer because she has to wait all night to appear, then she's only on stage for about five minutes. She gets no sympathy from the audience either.

Puccini was a man of the theatre. He wanted his opera to reflect life. Just as his mini-opera *Suor Angelica* takes about 20 minutes to really get going, presumably to reflect everyday life in the convent, so *Madama Butterfly* opens with the business of wedding preparations. The first violins play a really gutsy tune, which is repeated eight bars later by the second violins, joined by the violas (if they count correctly) eight bars later. Then the celli and double basses do their thing. It's an energetic piece of orchestral writing and one that perfectly leads us into the action.

The tenor, American naval officer Pinkerton – aka Lieutenant Linkerton if you hear it in German because the other spelling refers to something rude – is being shown around the house by Goro, a nasty character tenor. There are servants rushing everywhere, just like the opening of Act Two in *Der Rosenkavalier*, getting everything ready for the marriage ceremony. Goro is something like a cross between a marriage broker and a pimp. He looks after Cio Cio San, hangs around like a bad smell and has arranged the wedding for the American. Throughout the score we hear Pinkerton's name as either Benjamin Franklin Pinkerton, B.F. Pinkerton or F.B. Pinkerton. There's usually half an hour's discussion at the first rehearsal about which is correct. Whichever way, Pinkerton's out for a good time and, on this particular day, the Japanese girl fits the bill. We meet the lovely Suzuki, Cio Cio San's servant. She's always there when you need her. It's generally accepted that the better the Suzuki is, the better Cio Cio San looks! Ask any mezzo soprano …

Sharpless, the American consul in Nagasaki, is heard offstage. (Actually, you'll be lucky if you can hear him with the orchestra playing at full volume.) He's here to witness the ceremony, sing a duet and have a drink. Naturally, Puccini wrote him as a baritone. He's usually played by an older man, a sort of father figure, and he has to develop this for the following acts. He and Pinkerton toast 'America For Ever'. Puccini thought it cute to quote actual and well-known themes in his scores. He uses the whole of a Japanese tune, 'Sakura', and several other traditional melodies to give flavour to the score, especially in Act One, so there can be no question about where the opera is set. In the middle of this melodious duet, Pinkerton asks Sharpless 'Milk-Punch or Whisky?', in English. For years I thought it was a choice of three drinks. Puccini covers every topical detail in this work.

Behind the scenes there's an assistant conductor ready to lead a bunch of geishas and a prima donna into the entrance of Butterfly. Goro rushes onstage and that's their cue. The assistant conductor looks at the image of the real conductor on the nearby television monitor and anticipates his beat, because the sound takes a split second to arrive in the auditorium. 'Ah. Quanto cielo! Quanto mar!' (So much sky! So much sea!) sing the ladies of the chorus, followed by Butterfly's first line 'Ancora un passo or via' (I'm almost there). The composer has instructed Cio Cio San (aka Madama Butterfly) to sing her first 15 bars offstage and this includes some pretty glorious phrases of vocal delicacy. In real terms, because of the distance between the soprano and *her* audience, and because there's a huge orchestra playing, she has to sing her loudest. I've stood there while a number of sopranos 'honk' their best before appearing onstage for 'Amiche, io son vennta al richiamo d'amor!' (Friends, I am summoned by love!) all cute and innocent. On a few occasions sopranos have used expletives as they hear the slow tempi for their entrance. Cio Cio San greets everyone and sees her Pinkerton for the first time. She tells Sharpless of her family's poverty and that her father is dead. Now comes a treat. He asks her age. She makes him guess. He starts at ten. Is this crazy? He guesses again. This time twenty. All right. This is enough. She admits to fifteen (which, let's face it, stretches credibility with most sopranos who sing this role). The wedding party consists of the imperial high commissioner, the registrar and her relations. There's a sort of chorus where the gossipy relations bitch about Pinkerton. 'He was offered to me first,'

149

claims one cousin. Others chant that 'It'll end in divorce'. If only it were so happy an ending.

While being shown the house rented for their life together, Cio Cio San wants to show her future husband her collection of 'women's things'. Perfectly placed on a tray by the props girl are handkerchiefs, a pipe, a sash, a small clasp, a mirror, a fan, a pot of colour and a set of steak knives. Whoops, that's been replaced by a dagger. Added to the collection are the spirits of her ancestors now in the form of little puppet statues. This whole sequence takes some practice for the soprano. One soprano, known as a decent interpreter of the role, has her own personal tray of goodies that she takes from one production to the next regardless of the production's design. Another insisted on bringing her own and treated them as though she was washing dirty laundry. The worst possible story of this little moment came when a colleague was standing in for a sick Cio Cio San. Her Italian was quite good but instead of singing 'la pipa' (the pipe) she gave an extra consonant 'la pippa' (blow job). I think the Pinkerton suddenly took an interest in this new soprano.

Before the official ceremony begins, Cio Cio San tells Pinkerton that she plans to adopt a new religion and be a Christian wife. The wedding takes place but the drinks are interrupted by the appearance of her uncle, the Bonze. He's heard on the grapevine that she is to disown her family and religion and he's not happy. He renounces her and curses her with eternal damnation. The family flees, as they do in such cases, and Cio Cio San is left crying a river. This is an obvious place for a big love duet to happen and Puccini doesn't let us down. About ten minutes later, soprano and tenor are slowly walking towards the bedroom to consummate their wedding. They sing a combined high C and the music dies away as the curtain falls.

Act Two opens with Suzuki praying to Buddha and playing a prayer bell. A sad Cio Cio San relates Pinkerton's promise, which she wholeheartedly believes, that 'One fine day' he will return. It's a very touching three minutes. Of course, it is also one of the most famous of all opera arias and usually brings long applause. Sharpless arrives at the house and Cio Cio San, who now insists on being called Madama Pinkerton, is overjoyed. She takes no notice of anything Sharpless has to say and is intent on showing how 'Americanised' she's become. (This was before television too.) Soon after the wedding night Pinkerton left and promised to come back when the Robin Redbreasts return. It was an easy out for Pinkerton and Cio Cio San's naivety is running at full throttle. We, the audience, now understand that three years have passed.

Goro has tried every way to get Cio Cio San to forget the American and wed a rich guy called Prince Yamadori. He's the one in the fabulous costume who has just, by chance, come to personally offer his affection. 'To you I would swear everlasting faith,' he declares even though he's divorced all his previous wives. Cio Cio San is available because in Japanese opera law abandonment is equivalent to divorce. The music of this Yamadori scene is some of the most lavish and luxurious from the Puccini pen. Cio Cio San refuses his advances and he exits.

Sharpless takes out a letter from Pinkerton and tries to read it to Cio Cio San but her continuous interruptions prevent her from understanding the seriousness of its contents. He asks what she would do if Pinkerton was not to return and she responds, 'Either of two things: I could sing or die'. Before Sharpless is ushered out of the house, Cio Cio San brings in the child conceived on the wedding night, and appropriately named Trouble (my friends, right here in Nagasaki city). Puccini's librettist gave him the name of Dolore (Sorrow) but in most productions he is called Trouble.

Let me tell you, W.C. Fields was right: 'never work with animals or children'. Naturally, children look nice because they're young and cute but the audience apparently watches only them – and the little monsters know it. Usually, Trouble is kept out of the rehearsal room, in the care of a minder, until the very second he is required. (If we had our way, he'd be in a cage.) This first scene is not a hard acting call: he just has to be carried around by the soprano and sit where placed. Sometimes he is directed to sit and stand at various musical points but this expectation is seldom rewarded.

A sound effect of a ship's cannon is heard and Suzuki brings her mistress a telescope for a close-up view. Yes, it's the *Abraham Lincoln,* Pinkerton's ship. Both women are ecstatic and strew flower petals around the stage as they prepare for the arrival. Once the stage is totally covered in fake flowers all three prepare for the long wait. Outside we hear some humming. It's a tune we've heard already in the letter scene and is very familiar to modern audiences from the French musical *Les Misérables*. It's comforting to know that Puccini wrote the original, but the French boys put words to the tune.

That's the end of Act Two but in most performances it segues into Act Three, which is a short but exceedingly dramatic half-hour finale preceded by a passionate orchestral interlude. The music suggests the overnight wait, Cio Cio San's memory of the time with her husband and the sounds of early morning. From a very great distance (halfway out of the theatre usually) we hear the 'Heave ho!' of sailors followed by the chirping of birds. I've had a fun time running around the back of the stage blowing bird whistles, which you have to fill with water to make the noise during performances while Cio Cio San, Suzuki and the now fast asleep Trouble sit motionless on the stage, peering into the auditorium.

The orchestral mood settles and we know it's a new day. Butterfly and the child go off for a drink of water as we see the arrival of Pinkerton,

Sharpless and a new woman. This mezzo soprano has had to hang about the back of the stage during a trio and the tenor aria before making her first vocal sound. Her name is Kate Pinkerton and, yes, she's the new wife. Pinkerton feels remorse being back in the house and sings an aria about it, but departs anyway at the end, leaving Kate and Suzuki looking at each other. A minute passes and Cio Cio San returns to discover what's been going on. Kate wants to take Trouble back with them to America. Humbly Butterfly accepts Pinkerton's decision and decides to kill herself. She asks Kate to come back in half an hour to collect the child (and find out for herself what it's like to be a mother). Puccini crafted *the* most beautiful tune to complement these sad lyrics.

With all the volume of a thunder clap, the timpani pound away as Cio Cio San draws the blinds. She is just about ready for the hara kiri when Trouble runs back onstage into her embrace. Now, this is something that has to be directed to a musical cue, and rehearsed accordingly. Once, again at a major orchestral rehearsal, the cue happened but there was no sign of the child. There was a brief pause and the cue was repeated. No child. The stage manager went to the child, who was standing there in the place ready for his entrance, and asked why he didn't move. 'I don't like the music,' came the reply. The stage manager said, 'But you know the music and that it's the cue when you run on and hug the lady.' 'But I don't like the music!' After some consideration, the child was asked, 'Well, what would you like them to play instead?' In a meek voice the boy replied, 'Happy Birthday?'

During the embrace Cio Cio San sings her final great aria. It's big, it's loud and it's dramatic. A few times I've seen Trouble hold his breath and cover his ears to soften the pain of her volume. She urges him to go and play – 'Va, gioca! gioca!' – then puts the knife in her neck as stipulated in the hara kiri manual. As she dies she hears the voice of Pinkerton calling her name. It's very sad.

IL TROVATORE

WHEN A COMPOSER appears ready to push the boundaries and take the artform to a new level, the result is rarely commercially successful. Critics may proclaim it an artistic triumph but audiences will stay away in droves. As ticket-buyers are required to keep a show running, these creative gems frequently fall into oblivion. The next stage in their life comes a century later when they are rediscovered by a scholar and appreciated, by some, as an important key in the development of our musical culture.

Other composers take a different road, that of formula. Take the well-known hamburger food chains. They use different varieties of ingredients, their packaging and publicity is particular to their brand name and the customers have faith that they will deliver a certain standard every time. With few exceptions they look similar too. They have followed a respected recipe then added a few personal touches. With all due respect, that is what

Giuseppe Verdi did when he wrote *Il Trovatore*. Let me explain.

Looking at the structure of the work, we see four distinct acts each divided into two or more scenes. Within every scene appears at least one aria plus a duet or ensemble. Each solo aria is preceded by a recitative and followed by a cabaletta (or faster section) supported by a jaunty orchestral accompaniment. All this is absolutely standard for an Italian opera of the early 1800s. With *Il Trovatore* in 1853, Verdi gave the audience exactly what they were expecting. Mind you, his genius would give any opera an immense boost.

If anyone tells you they know the plot of *Il Trovatore,* don't believe them. The storyline is absolutely ludicrous and is as contrived as the jewel operettas of W.S. Gilbert and Arthur Sullivan. Indeed, Gilbert was obviously influenced by Verdi's work when writing *The Gondoliers* in 1889. The parallels between *Il Trovatore* and *The Gondoliers* are obvious – twin boys stolen at birth from an aristocratic family and an old gypsy who confesses before the final curtain that she mixed them at birth.

When the curtain goes up on the first scene of the opera we are outside the apartments of Count di Luna. Assembled are the full male choristers and a secondary bass character named Ferrando, who's the captain of the guard. Late at night the men are waiting to nab the short tenor who's been serenading the prima donna outside her window.

The girl happens to be Donna Leonora, a noble lady in the Court of Aragon. If you haven't already guessed, we are in 15th-century Spain. While waiting for the tenor, who never appears in this scene, Ferrando (at the request of the other soldiers) sings an aria to us and the male chorus, who describe the tale leading to this moment in the story. It's a gruesome narrative about the Count's brother. I won't bother to tell you it here because it's retold by one of the principal singers in Act Two, and I don't want to spoil the effect. I don't understand why Verdi and his librettists gave this moment to the bass, and so early in the opera too. Anyway, Verdi supplies him with a jaunty tune in 3/4 time that would make the score instantly accessible to the audience of the day. Perhaps this was part of Verdi's genius?

Next scene is in the gardens of the palace. Supported by some 'lurking' chords in the orchestra, Leonora is anxiously waiting for something to happen in her life, followed at three paces by her maid Inez. The latter is usually an older female singer, soprano or mezzo. We gather that Leonora is captivated by an unknown knight whom she crowned victor at some competitions a little while ago. He's been pestering her ever since by singing under her window. She tells us this in an emotionally uneasy aria, 'Tacea la notte placida' (The night calmly and peacefully in beauty seemed reposing) and then, after a brilliant cadenza, immediately follows it with a cabaletta filled with staccato and trills. For the soprano, this is usually the hardest part of the role to sing. Verdi wrote mostly long phrases for Leonora and these bits of vocal needlepoint seem to be written for another sort of singer. She and Inez leave during the applause.

One time, working on a production of this opera, we had a soprano who was not beloved of her cast or crew members. She was young, tall and loud but had no sense of the qualities that make this role great. In the costume – a huge crinoline skirt – she won the name of 'the singing lounge chair'. Her Inez was a short mezzo. Attired in a similar crinoline she looked remarkably like a Fiat Bambino. It was an engrossing image for the audience.

Same scene but a little later in the night: Count di Luna comes into the garden and sings some recitative and is about to sing an aria about the loveliness of Leonora. Suddenly he is interrupted by the sounds of an offstage harp. We are meant to believe that it's a lute played by the troubadour of our opera's title but you'd never hear such a soft instrument from backstage. Manrico, the troubadour, serenades Leonora with two verses. On stage, Count di Luna, the principal baritone, is left to his own devices to keep the visual interest while the aural interest is elsewhere. In between verses he mumbles a few words so we know that he's still there.

Finally something happens in the plot. Leonora rushes into the garden ready to greet her admirer and, in the darkness of the night, believes Count di Luna to be that person. With the change in moon, Leonora sees the figure of a masked cavalier, recognises it as that of her lover, Manrico, and turns from the Count di Luna. Manrico discloses his identity and the men draw their swords. This cues a trio which vibrantly closes Act One with the soprano and tenor sailing up to a high D flat.

In the next scene we discover the old gypsy Azucena huddled over a fire. Fairly soon we realise that she's the central focus of this opera and story but first we hear the famous 'Anvil Chorus', in which the gypsies swing their hammers and bring them down on clanking metal in rhythm with the music. It's as primeval an action as clanging your cutlery while waiting for dinner – and equally entertaining. Music staff are usually in the wings both sides of the stage having a wonderful time nearly breaking their arms competing for the loudest clang. The noise leaves a ringing in your ears for several hours afterwards. This is segued by Azucena's famous 'Stride la vampa' (Upward the flames roll). It is an aria in E minor with the mezzo's vocal line pulsating over the unbending string accompaniment. In this aria, Azucena sings of her memories and hatreds as she relates the story of her mother's death. When the aria is over she adds, 'Mi vendica!' (Avenge me!). This is the first suggestion that there'll be tears before bedtime. In any case, the chorus exit the scene singing a reprise of their anvil tune.

Azucena is a gift of a role for any performer. Even if she manages only to sing the notes and words, Verdi's masterly writing and theatrical power will give the audience enough to sense the greatness of her character. On the exceedingly rare occasions when the role is performed by a complete singing actor, the result is mind-blowing. Sad to say, I long for the day when I see another great Azucena on stage.

In the early 1980s, the English director Elijah Moshinsky was faced with a cast that included a treasured mezzo soprano with only basic dramatic skills. In a flash of brilliance, he made her sit through the whole first scene in a throne-like chair. That way the audience would be focused on her vocal presence rather than her lack of theatrical presence. Her stillness drew the audience in and gave her strength. She had a triumph that season.

A few years later, the production was revived with an Italian mezzo soprano performing her signature role, Azucena. She listened to the direction with a smile and did her own thing as soon as the curtain went up. She got out of that chair as soon as possible and never returned. She was all over the front of the stage, eating the set, as they say. Strangely she wasn't invited back!

Left alone, Azucena furthers her story with a narrative that is one of the most famous moments for an operatic mezzo soprano. (Verdi had toyed with the idea of calling the opera *Azucena*.) In a terrifyingly vivid retelling of the story Ferrando told us in the first scene of Act One, Azucena relives every second of her 'terrible secret'. (In opera, gypsies always have terrible secrets.) It turns out that Azucena's mother was accused of witchcraft by the evil Count di Luna and burnt at the stake, on the same spot where the gypsies now have their camp. This is operatic coincidence. As her mother called out 'Mi vendica! Mi vendica!' (Avenge me!) – the same words we've heard only a few minutes ago – Azucena grabbed one of the Count's twin baby sons and hurled him into the burning flames. The only problem was that she obviously had poor eyesight and threw her own baby into the fire. In any case, Azucena decided to bring the other child up as her own. This tale of vengeance arouses doubts in Manrico's mind as to whether he really is her son.

Did I not tell you the plot was crazy?

Manrico and his adopted mother sing a duet, 'Mal reggendo all' aspro assalto' (Ill sustaining the furious encounter), telling why he did not kill Count di Luna at the end of Act One. When the Count's life was his for a single thrust, a voice from heaven bade him spare it, suggesting that Manrico unconsciously was swayed by the relationship. This is a touch of psychology rare in Italian opera librettos and most unexpected in this particular work.

Enter now the messenger Ruiz, a character tenor, who orders Manrico to take command of the forces defending the stronghold of Castellor.

Ruiz adds that Leonora believes Manrico to be dead and is about to take the veil in a convent near the castle.

The scene changes: the Count and his followers in the cloister of the convent. He plans to carry off Leonora before she becomes a nun and sings of his love for her in a beautiful aria, 'Il balen del suo sorriso' (Of her smile, the radiant gleaming). Ferrando and the male choristers join him in a martial type cabaletta, 'Per me ora fatale' (O, fatal hour impending) and they hide.

Things start to hot up. A chorus of nuns is heard offstage. Leonora, Inez and her ladies enter and are about to proceed from the cloister into the convent when they are startled by the appearance of the Count. Before he can seize Leonora, another figure stands between them. It's Manrico. With him are Ruiz and his followers. It's time for a great ensemble. Leonora starts with 'E deggio! – e posso crederlo?' (And can I still my eyes believe!) as she looks at Manrico who she had thought was dead. Manrico, the Count di Luna and full chorus sing their hearts out as the Act Two curtain swiftly moves us to interval drinks.

Act Three opens with another lively chorus to get you back into the mood of what story is left. We are in the province of the Count di Luna. The soldiers have captured Azucena and drag her in. When questioned by the Count, she sings that she is just a poor wanderer. Ferrando recognises her as the gypsy who, to avenge her mother, threw the infant brother of the Count into the flames. She cries out to Manrico to come to her rescue. This further enrages the Count. He orders that she be cast into prison and then burnt at the stake.

After a brief change of scenery, we discover Leonora and Manrico awaiting their marriage vows. He sings a gorgeous aria, 'Ah sì, ben mio, coll'essere' (Ah yes, you are my wife by right) to her and they harmonise a duet filled with young love. Just as Manrico takes Leonora's hand to lead her to the altar of the chapel, Ruiz rushes in with word that Azucena has been captured and is about to be killed. The glow of flames can already be seen. Manrico draws his sword, and sings the great testosterone-filled cabaletta 'Di quella pira l'orrendo foco' (See the pyre blazing, o sight of horror), and rushes out to attempt to save his mother from the barbecue.

This celebrated moment can be encored. Although it's not written in the printed score, audiences expect the tenor to end the number with a long high C. It's important that the tenor's face change to bright purple as he sings it otherwise the audience won't realise that it's a difficult note to sing. Several tenors I've witnessed have saved their energies for a dozen bars before they launch their attempt at the 'money note'. A couple of times, I've seen a chorister with a 'freak' high C stand close to the Manrico and, at the given moment, bellow it as the tenor mimes. The audience never knew. The prized Italian tenor, Franco Bonisolli, had high Cs galore and would hold this note for ages – until after the orchestra had finished. Then he would hungrily accept the cheers from the rent-a-crowd (or claque) and punch out those who booed.

Act Four contains some of the most memorable music in the operatic repertoire. As the curtain goes up we prepare ourselves for a performance of a divine lyric soprano aria from Verdi's pen. Finally alone, Leonora sends her thoughts to Manrico whose defence of Castellor failed and is currently offstage in jail. This aria, 'D'amor sull ali rosee' (On rosy wings of love depart) is one that only a diva can perform in the approved manner. The vocal phrases soar to the high reaches of the soprano range and they must be sung with style, finesse and, above all else, beauty of soul.

Against a sombre 'Miserere' chanted by an offstage chorus, Leonora sings of her need to have Manrico released from jail. In another area of the wings, Manrico bemoans his fate. Two solos and a backing chorus piece together to form a great piece of music theatre. Even when you're backstage conducting the tenor, you still get goosebumps at the end of this ensemble.

The Count di Luna confronts Leonora and she promises to become his wife if he will free Manrico. Of course, the Count agrees. Unbeknown to him, Leonora has a ring filled with poison. She turns away from him, drinks its contents and sings to the audience, 'M'avrai, ma fredda esanime spoglia' (A cold and lifeless corpse he'll find me). Nevertheless, they sing a big duet about it.

In another piece of operatic coincidence, Manrico and Azucena find themselves together in chains in the final scene. They use the moment to sing a duet, 'Ai nostri monti' (Home to our mountains).

A frustrated Leonora enters and bids him escape but Manrico knows better. As a sleeping Azucena croons the tune of the duet, the two lovers find themselves minutes away from death – Leonora from the poison and Manrico from the executioner's axe. She expires as do many Verdi sopranos, a few pages from the end and Count di Luna drags Azucena to the window to witness the death of her supposed son.

'It is over!' exclaims the Count.

'The victim was your brother!' cries Azucena gleefully. 'Mother, you are avenged!'

There ends the silliest opera plot of them all – but what a wonderful score.

THE BARITONE

OPERATIC BARITONES CAN be conceited, pompous and egotistical creatures. I don't mean to appear uncaring but, all things considered, these men are a breed unto themselves. Perhaps it is the fact that they are regularly cast as despised or villainous characters that makes them so needy offstage. Now and again, however, they are someone's brother or husband and in a few cases, a baritone will get the girl.

Escamillo certainly does (but for how long will he last with Carmen?) and Marcello is reunited with Musetta in *La Bohème* (but no one cares – by then the story is totally focused on Mimi and Rodolfo). Salome gets the baritone – well, actually only his head. On the operatic stage, the baritone is obsessed with the soprano. Whether it is that Verdi's Rigoletto cares for the safety of his daughter, Scarpia needs to own Tosca, Valentine in Gounod's *Faust* has a devout love for his sister Marguerite, Germont Pere in Verdi's *La Traviata* destroys the relationship between his son and Violetta, the title character in Tchaikovsky's *Eugene Onegin* can't commit to a relationship with Tatyana or the love of Senta is desperately needed to bring Wagner's Flying Dutchman final peace, it is the plight of the baritone to endure rejection.

Baritones come in various shapes and sizes. God kept the attribute of height for the bass and contralto so it's quite common to find celebrated baritones who are short in stature and dwarfed by their co-stars while singing the big 'macho' roles in the repertoire. I am reminded of a handful of occasions where the baritone sang his entire role from a place higher on the stage set just to make him appear taller – or as tall – as the rest of the cast.

My first job on a production of *Rigoletto* was playing the thunder sheet in Act Three. Just after the famous quartet 'Bella figlia dell'amore', there's a suggestion that a storm is about to start. Two levels below the stage, in what is called the dock, where the stage sets and scenery are stored, was housed a piece of iron about a metre wide and many metres long with a wooden edge attached to the bottom. It hung from the ceiling to about mid-body height so that a member of the music staff could 'play' it when required in the score. This meant shaking it from the bottom like a huge wobble board. The effect was like a rumble of thunder. One could gradate the velocity of the action to make it sound louder or longer. A sharp jerk gave the effect of a thunder clap. This was wild stuff and I thought I was really the star of the show. The conductor and director gave me precise instructions on when it should be played and how it should sound. Once I achieved perfection in my part I never changed my performance.

As this manual sound effect happens only towards the end of Verdi's opera, I would only be required to come to the theatre 30 minutes beforehand so I never heard the beginning of the opera. Offstage drama abounded one Saturday matinée. The scheduled baritone was ill. His understudy was even sicker. Management called every baritone in the country – they even had one on stand-by to sing the role in English – but none was game to risk his reputation. That morning I was playing piano accompaniment for a student's lesson at the studio of a famous baritone. The phone rang and we noticed a delighted smile appear on his face. He said, 'Just a minute', came to the piano keyboard and played a high G, took a good breath and produced the loudest and ugliest noise we'd heard up to that point in our careers. He strutted back to the waiting telephone and said, 'Okay. I'll be there'. The lesson came to an abrupt end and we helped him look for his vocal score. After a few fraught moments he said, 'It's all right. I know it perfectly without a score.' What we, and the management, didn't know was that he hadn't sung the role for over 15 years.

Of course, I scurried early to the theatre and

stood in the wings to watch history unfold. I was surprised to see the baritone, now in full costume and makeup, chatting to the choristers, laughing and renewing old acquaintances. A prompt box was added for this matinée but the baritone instructed the prompt that he only ever needed cueing at three small places …

The dim tones of the prelude started in the orchestra pit, the curtain went up, the tenor sang his jaunty 'Questo e quella' and the cue for Rigoletto's entrance came. There he was smiling from ear to ear, ready to launch back into his career. What we experienced was like watching a train crash. Nothing was right. He made up every word, every note and movement. Thankfully that first scene isn't too big a sing for Rigoletto and the rest of the cast sang their lines no matter what was coming out of his mouth. The scene goes straight into the slimy scene with Sparafucile, through Rigoletto's aria-type recitative 'Pari siamo' and on to the big duet with Gilda. The look on the soprano's face was indescribable as she wondered what would next confront her.

There wasn't much talk backstage during the interval. The conductor of that particular performance later told me that he went to his room, locked the door and prayed. He promised that he'd change his life, give up alcohol and women if only something would put an end to this musical and theatrical calamity. After the usual 15 minutes he heard his call to return to the orchestra pit. The second, and final call came three minutes later. He placed his hands on the doorknob to leave his dressing room and suddenly everything became dark. Originally the conductor thought that he'd died or, at least, passed out. Over the tannoy speakers he heard the emergency drill advising that, owing to an electrical fault, the performance would not continue. A drill on a nearby construction site had cut through the electrical cables.

That was the end of the show and there was jubilation backstage. Everyone was pleased the trauma would be ended, including the baritone. For the rest of his life, he told everyone with the utmost pride that he'd sung Rigoletto 500 and a half times. Were the other 500 performed in his living room?

In a recent interview, a greatly admired Spanish baritone Carlos Alvarez was quoted as saying that being a Verdi baritone these days 'is like being a one-eyed man in a kingdom of the blind'. No truer words have been said. Fashion states that singers today must be versatile, capable of singing roles from Mozart, Handel and Verdi to modern repertoire. Specialising in a certain type of role can limit a career and baritones who used to sing only the meaty roles of the Italian school are now asked to sing roles such as Rossini's Figaro as well. Voice teachers start a student on Mozart and Handel without the knowledge that it's easier to train a voice with good Verdi. It's sad that we now have to endure Mozart baritones singing Verdi without the vocal heft or stylish swagger demanded. Today, many a Papageno voice has a perfectly good career singing the Flying Dutchman.

One singer I greatly admire has developed his voice and technique to encompass the middle Verdi roles, and he performs them with distinction. An admired Rigoletto, Macbeth, Count di Luna, Ford and Nabucco, he approaches each new role with intelligence. He loves to ask questions in rehearsals, likes to display his knowledge and gets in a bad mood when things change. His ego makes him unpopular with his colleagues. Many years ago, he was performing an early Verdi role under a conductor whose 40-year career had taken him to the greatest opera houses in the world and he'd worked with the most famous of singers. During a rather important stage rehearsal – these moments usually happen at important times – we were reading through a key scene with the baritone and chorus. The usually quite humble maestro stopped several times to give musical corrections and suggestion notes to the baritone. After what must have been the sixth pause in his rehearsal, the baritone, petulant, pouting and defiant, stopped, looked directly at the maestro on the podium and launched into a ramble that included the phrase 'Never in my career'. Each time he repeated 'my career' the words became more theatrically stressed. He ended his rant and there was a brief pause. In a perfectly enunciated voice the maestro asked 'What career?' As a sense of satisfaction blossomed on the faces of the chorus, the baritone looked at the ground and the rehearsal proceeded.

The great (well, experienced) Italian conductor Nello Santi told me of the first time he conducted *La Traviata*. It was in the very early 1950s. He was young but his knowledge of repertoire was brilliant. The provincial Italian theatre was tiny, about the size of a local pub. Such a small auditorium can bring the intimacy of the performance to new heights. Germont Père makes his grand entrance in Act Two. Just before the act was about to begin, the stage manager told Maestro Santi that the baritone singing Germont had just dropped dead in his dressing room. An announcement was made front of curtain stating that the contracted baritone was 'unable to perform' but management would be able to locate a substitute within the hour – there are singers aplenty in Italy. The audience was requested to take a long dinner break and the performance would resume in an hour or so. As would be expected in the country where opera is close to the heart of every citizen, chaos erupted, but they did as they were told and went off for a meal and vino. Sure enough, an elderly baritone was found and agreed to save the evening for a large fee – as well as insisting that the 'traditional cuts' in the score were employed. Santi, without realising what he was getting himself into, accepted. No one remembered that the aged baritone had an axe to grind with previous management. Act Two started.

On stepped Germont Père and delivered his famous first line, 'Madamigella Valéry?', in a somewhat husky voice. The soprano responded with her line 'Son io' and then Germont delivered an enormous cut of about eight minutes of music, the pages that contain the crux of the story. He sang 'addio', then left the stage! The audience had a field day.

There are some great roles in the repertoire for lighter voiced baritones who also look good. Throughout operatic history it's generally been the tenor who thrills your ears but it's the baritone who melts your heart. The celebrity baritones Lawrence Tibbett and John Charles Thomas in the 1930s were prime examples of this. On radio, Nelson Eddy excited a large number of female listeners. Tibbett and Eddy were fine-looking film actors as well as enjoying careers on the opera stage, although the latter's opera career ended when he went into movies. In the past two decades, the opera world has publicised baritone hunks like Thomas Hampson (did you hear that his Christmas CD was going to be called '*O Come Let Them Adore Me*'?), Nathan Gunn and Teddy Tahu Rhodes. You might note that almost every role they do includes a scene where they remove their shirt to expose a six-pack. From the title role in Britten's *Billy Budd* to the pivotal role in Jake Heggie's recent opera *Dead Man Walking*, there is a good handful of opportunities where a baritone can disrobe to please the audience.

I was fortunate to be part of a season of Verdi's

Otello early on in my career. Two baritones shared the role of Iago, the guy who spoils everything. Long-time colleagues, they started their careers around 1950 and, although their paths didn't cross for some decades, they ended up in Australia competing for roles over the last 20 years of their performing lives. They played golf together and had a similar circle of friends, but never really liked each other. Underneath the bluster and jovial repartee lay a seething competitive streak. As they had both been my idols when I was a youngster, it was fascinating to watch them perform in alternating shows during the season. Iago makes his entrance fairly early in Act One and sings a brindisi (a drinking song) to encourage Cassio to get drunk. Each verse ends with a 'Bevi, bevi' that goes up to a high A – not too easy for a baritone. In these difficult phrases, the aged singers strove to outdo each other. I have never heard better, louder, more supported high A's from any baritone before or since. These artists were in their 60s and still showing the younger generation how to do it but they were not pleased when I asked which one was the understudy.

DON GIOVANNI

AS MUCH AS I like to stir the pot and make people think about why an operatic work is a masterpiece, I must agree with those academics who loudly state that Mozart's *Don Giovanni* is the perfect opera.

It's a sad admission but I'm sorry to add that, in all my years working in the industry, I've never been completely satisfied by a single production or cast of this opera. Why? Mozart has crafted a brilliant score filled with melody and theatre. Lorenzo da Ponte's text is so articulate that one could easily perform the libretto with straight actors and enjoy the theatrical experience. So why is it affectionately known as the director's nightmare? Rather than trust the work to play itself, directors feel the need to inject something interesting into a piece that is already interesting enough. There are unlimited operas that need rejigging – Mozart's penultimate opera, *La Clemenza di Tito,* for example – giving opportunities to a clever director. In my opinion, there's no need to tamper with *Don Giovanni* because everything most audiences want in a performance is already there in abundance. Moss Hart once said, 'You don't have to be different to be good. Being good is different enough.'

The opera's complete title is *Il Dissoluto Punito, ossia il Don Giovanni* (translated as *The Rake Punished, or Don Giovanni*) and its subject must surely have been rather risqué when it was premiered in Prague on 29 October 1787. First, the plot is inspired by the well-known story of Casanova or Don Juan, the great lover whose reputed sexual conquests were famous and many. *Don Giovanni*'s brilliant librettist chose not to depict any of these conquests during the action of this work, preferring to depict him as a sexy loser. Try as Don Giovanni might, something or someone always appears at the wrong moment to put a spanner in the works. Take for example the opening scene of the opera. The Don – as we'll call him hereafter – is first seen by the audience attempting to rape Donna Anna, a Spanish noblewoman, in her boudoir. In a recent American production, the bare butt of the baritone was the first thing the patrons saw as the curtain rose. Sadly his vocal tone was not as rounded. The role of Donna Anna is best sung by a dramatic soprano because when she says 'No', she really means it.

The Don's butler, Leporello, waits outside to join his master in a quick escape. He complains about his job, as most manservants do. As the energy of the orchestra quickly builds, Anna escapes the Don's clutches, races out of the bedroom and hurls an avalanche of abuse at her assailant. Their vocal energies blend at such a volume as to waken Anna's father, the Commendatore. After a couple of bars he works out what's happening and draws his sword to kill the intruder. Mozart wrote a speedy eight bars of melodrama music to support the onstage action. As you'd expect, the Don quickly runs his sword through the father's chest. Naturally, an 'Ah, I'm dying' trio is sung by all three men on stage – Don Giovanni, Leporello and the Commendatore.

Next we have the first taste of recitative for the evening. Our Latin lover is obviously shaken from the incident. This recitative, or sung dialogue, must be performed as a whisper to keep the mood of the drama. I hate hearing recitative performed as though it's the next aria.

I need not chat about each individual scene in the opera. Suffice to say that the Don encounters three women in this opera. He offers his services to each of them but the only person who wants him is a dead male – and he is after his soul.

We're introduced first to Donna Anna, who managed to escape the Don in the opening scene. Her boyfriend is a feeble chap called Don Ottavio. Actually, Ottavio is a wonderful role and has been performed by the greatest tenors of history, but when he's badly presented as a character, the audience thinks he's a wimp. Throughout the plot

Anna and Ottavio do their best to bring the Don to his knees. Initially they have a fine duet in which Anna realises that her father is dead. Later there's a grand moment that involves an extended accompanied dramatic recitative (with orchestra) for Anna, while Ottavio looks on, followed by a high aria where she swears vengeance on the Don. Might I add that Mozart gives Don Ottavio a meltingly beautiful aria, 'Dalla sua pace' (On her, all joy depends) to sing as soon as Anna's applause has died away. This little aria is often omitted, sometimes for good reason. Written in the key of G major, it sits right in the vocal break of the tenor voice. Tenors find it difficult to sustain the high tessitura and have been known to sing it very under pitch. In Act Two, Ottavio has a second aria, with long coloratura phrases that should be sung on a single breath. 'Il mio tesoro intanto' (To my beloved), which has an attractive tune that is rhythmically boppy, is in the concert repertoire of most tenors of worth.

Donna Elvira, sung by either soprano or mezzo soprano, is a crazy mixed-up girl, not particularly liked by anyone on stage. Very few mezzos have achieved success with the role as it sits high in the voice – possibly to suggest her frenzy. She has really only one aria and that's in Act Two. Like Ottavio's 'Dalla sua pace', Elvira's 'Mi tradi quell'alma ingrata' (You have betrayed me, cruel heart) is frequently cut from performance and I suggest that, if a mezzo is singing the role, you cover your ears at this point in the evening. This aria is a rant. Her voice is supposed to blend with a solo clarinet weaving in and out, like playing games. Mezzos have great difficulty getting through the aria. You can guess that I prefer a soprano in the role.

Elvira can be a great role if it's performed by an artist of delicacy and good comic timing. Her entrance can steal the show. In that initial scene we see her nag the Don after neither recognises the other. He had left her high and dry in a recent tryst, never fulfilling his promise to return to her. We can understand his reluctance when we hear her frenzied appeals. After the Don has exited stage left, Elvira gets to 'act' when Leporello produces a little black book that lists all of Don Giovanni's conquests. Her eyes roll when Leporello quotes 640 in Italy, 520 in France and 200 in Germany. They absolutely bulge when Spain boasts 1003. When did he get the time? How did he access that amount of Viagra?

We meet the new girl in the story about a third of the way through Act One. Zerlina is a peasant girl, a charming creature who has innocence and youth on her side. She and her fiancé Masetto, a boy with attitude, enter with the chorus (who play a very small part in this opera) and are soon introduced to the Don. Zerlina is new to his menu and he immediately offers to show her his etchings back at his casinetto. Naiveté is a great thing when you're a young soprano or mezzo – again, Zerlina can be sung by either – and they sing the well-known duet of seduction 'La ci darem la mano' (Give me your hand). Just as they leave the stage in the duet's rhythmic coda, Elvira stops them in their tracks and starts another onslaught. Later Zerlina has two charming arias. The first, 'Batti, batti, o bel Masetto' (Beat me, beat me, dear Masetto) enjoys a cello obbligato running through its second half; the Act Two aria 'Vedrai, carino' (You will see, my dear) comforts her betrothed after he's been bashed by the Don. With the magic of Mozart's pen, the comfort comes quickly.

Leporello, the manservant/butler to our title character is a buffo bass baritone. He is a bit like Don Bartolo in Rossini's *Il Barbiere di Siviglia* and is frequently sung by a similar performer. He has a lot of patter in his two arias – especially in the famous catalogue song he sings to Donna Elvira – but his main function is to provide charm and personality. These two aspects of performance are also essential for the baritone playing Don Giovanni. Sure, he must be able to sing the notes with a good sound, but the audience must find him spunky and adorable. His physique and elegance should complement Mozart's articulate vocal line and da Ponte's absolute gift of a libretto. The great Dons of operatic history have included all the drop-dead gorgeous celebrity baritones. In the distant past Ezio Pinza and Cesare Siepi, both Italian born, excelled in every aspect of the role. Pinza had great legs too – he was a professional bike-rider in his youth – and all the girls loved Siepi. His Don fame was so great that in 1962 he starred in a Broadway musical titled *Bravo Giovanni*. The music had nothing to do with Mozart and even included a song called 'The Kangaroo', so I presume that da Ponte had nothing to do with it either.

Perhaps the first character we meet musically is the Commendatore, Anna's father. Those thunderous D minor chords in the first bar of the overture suggest not only the Don's eventual fate but the warning not to cross the father of a soprano. The bass appears four times in the opera. We meet him in his dressing gown, angry at being awoken from his snooze. About three minutes later he's lying on stage *morto* (dead). He then waits in his dressing room ready to appear in the middle of Act Two as the statue of the Commendatore – in appropriate stone make-up. He materialises above his grave and sings two phrases with sinister trombone accompaniment – it's an eerie effect that really works – while the Don and Leporello converse in recitative.

The continuo player (the harpsichordist) is responsible for keeping the recitative in place. Years ago, in my first *Don Giovanni* away from home, we had the delight of a Don and Leporello who arrived without seeming to have learnt their roles. During the rehearsal weeks it was obvious that neither was inclined to commit any of the recitative to memory. Their onstage colleagues had problems of their own. The Anna and Elvira were ill cast and, through no fault of their own, looked and sang like buxom truck-drivers. (One went on to sing the major Wagner roles internationally; the other's career went nowhere.) The Don and Leporello faked the music and made up the recitative. Unfortunately, as I was seated at the harpsichord, I had to follow and support their textual and musical recomposition. I doubt whether many members of the audience knew it but the scene in the cemetery was complete gobbledygook every night.

I forgot to mention that, during that scene, the pompous Don Giovanni invites the statue of the Commendatore to join him at dinner that evening. Surprising no one, the statue accepts the invitation and arrives as planned while the Don is feasting away. This final scene has the quaint addition of an onstage band that plays quotes of tunes from some of Mozart's contemporaries, including Jose Soler's *La Cosa Rara*, a very popular opera of the time. Best of all is when we hear a few bars of Mozart's own 'Non piu andrai' from *The Marriage of Figaro* and the Don sings, 'That's a tune I've heard too often'. Neurotic Elvira makes a brief entrance, chaos breaks out and the statue arrives, announced by the same thunderous chords from the first page of the overture. He asks for Don Giovanni's hand. Foolishly he gives it and the statue drags him down to hell, sometimes through a trapdoor in the floor of the stage. There's a wonderful story of the trapdoor getting stuck as the statue and the Don were halfway down. Someone in the audience shouted out with joy, 'Praise the Lord. Hell's full!'

The opera could stop there but Mozart and Da Ponte chose to add an epilogue in which Anna, Elvira, Zerlina, Ottavio, Leporello and Masetto sing the moral of the story: he who wrought for selfish pleasure shall depart without a friend.

Singers are notorious for having short bladders. While waiting in the wings for their entrance, they'll rush to the toilet to empty one last drop. The bass performing the Commendatore was in his statue disguise in the cemetery scene. The stage set had the grave monument design covering the statue's waist, with only his face and torso seen by the audience. Of course, he forgot to pee before this longish scene of absolute stillness. Thinking that no one would notice, he decided to take a leak onstage. Nature took its course and a trickle of liquid quickly emerged from below the Commendatore's grave and made its way down the raked stage, heading directly for the prompter's box. Anticipating the inevitable, she caught the yellow river with her pointer finger and directed it around the side of the box, where it finished its journey in the orchestra pit. I never heard the next part of that story … Most disturbing is the thought that she had to continue the rest of the performance without washing her finger. Did the conductor shake her hand at the curtain calls?

In fact, many of the weirdest moments I've

encountered in rehearsals have happened during a *Don Giovanni* production. One afternoon, while on tour, we returned to the rehearsal space after the lunch break to find heavy chains and padlocks on the doors. The reason? The owner of the building had forgotten to pay his mortgage for several months and the bank had decided to bring in the bailiffs. The next day we were rehearsing in a different venue.

Perhaps the most bizarre story comes from a colleague who invited a young academic as his guest to a performance of this powerful opera. The student was so enthused by the performance that he stood up at the final curtain and cried out, 'Author, author!'

FAUST

FOR SEVERAL DECADES, Gounod's *Faust* fell out of favour with audiences. Whether it was because of its immense popularity in the 19th century or its incredibly tuneful score, it was deemed old-fashioned until 20 years ago, when opera companies rediscovered this masterpiece. In the current repertoire it almost shares pride of place as the most popular French opera with Bizet's *Carmen* – and that is saying something. Whether the piece lives or dies on stage depends on the way it is presented to modern audiences. In the old days, sometimes even today, the opera was set in 15th century Germany and everyone was running around in pigtails, plaits and tights. Furthermore, it was convention that Méphistophélès, the devil character, wear red leg tights along with the rest of his costume. If you've ever seen the legs on a bass you'd understand why this was gag material.

The opera was premiered in Paris in 1859 and was an immediate success. Unlike so many other instant hits, it remained successful and many of the greatest singers of the time were featured in its principal roles. It takes artists of real calibre to make these characters real to a modern audience, and updating the period of the setting can help with this.

The story of Dr Faustus is centuries old. An old philosopher, Faust, trades his soul for the return of his youth but unfortunately makes his bargain with the devil, Méphistophélès, and things do not go as expected.

Act One starts fairly gloomily in Faust's study. Not a young man, he's disillusioned with everything in life and is about to kill himself. In some productions he's dabbling in black magic and that's how the director manages the appearance of Méphistophélès. In his heavily depressed state Faust, a tenor, dreams of the farmers harvesting grain outside and of the virginal girls out there with them. Just as he's about to end it all there's a big chord in the orchestra and the bass appears in a puff of smoke. He introduces himself in a charismatic way and asks what would make Faust happy. It's not wealth or fame because Faust already has these. He desires youth (who doesn't?) and agrees to sign the contract described above. A simple extreme makeover might have been easier. As a bonus Méphistophélès shows Faust the image of a very beautiful girl who will feature heavily in the story, Marguerite is a vision of loveliness. Usually the soprano playing this role is garbed in a glamourous costume and surrounded by careful lighting. I remember a production that had her in a sexy backless gown – a bit like the famous Marlene Dietrich costume – with bugle beads in clusters just covering the nipples. It took courage for the soprano to venture onto the stage, let alone into the corridor leading to the stage, in this sparse outfit. It looked great and all was well until the revival the following year. That cast included a well-loved soprano who had been performing Marguerite for 30 years. She looked good in most respects, but parts of her physique weren't up to this bare-all gown so she insisted on wearing a bra. From the front it seemed okay but all was not well at the back ... The lighting designer assisted by dimming the lights when she appeared.

Faust, overjoyed, drinks a potion, flings off his old costumes and dons the fashion of a man in the full blush of youth as he and Méphistophélès sing an energetic duet. That's Act One.

We next find ourselves at a town fair. Individual groups of choristers sing and finally join together for a big ending. The women and children depart and we're left with a group of men drinking in a tavern. A troubled-looking guy appears holding a medallion. We quickly learn that it's Marguerite's brother Valentin, who is about to go to war. The medallion was her gift to him to bring him good luck. She shouldn't have bothered, as we'll learn in about an hour and a half. The aria he sings is one of the standard baritone numbers that we frequently hear at concerts, 'Avant de quitter ces lieux' (Before leaving this place – otherwise known as 'Even bravest hearts'). Charles Gounod knew the power of a good tune and he included this one in the overture just so we'd like it more the second time we heard it. One of the most memorable performances I experienced was at the Bastille Opera in Paris. A short man with no personality walked on stage, stood there displaying little charm and sang this aria like a god! He finished the scene and walked off as though he'd read the grocery list. Unbelievable.

Valentin is followed around by two friends – Wagner, a baritone who has almost nothing to sing in the opera and Siebel, who is a mezzo soprano dressed as a boy. Siebel is one of Faust's students and he's in love with Marguerite. After a couple of minutes drinking stage beer Wagner decides it's time to sing 'The Song of the Rat', a piece of no quality whatsoever. He's interrupted after a few bars by Méphistophélès, who shows that he can sing longer and louder than them all. His choice of tune is 'Le veau d'or' (The Song of the Golden Calf). It's two verses of pelvic swirling rhythm that invigorates the assembled players, who lustily join in singing the chorus. Having won the cast over with this vocal display, Méphistophélès tells each character's fortune: 'Valentin will be killed, Siebel will have trouble with wilting flowers and Wagner...who cares?' He then toasts Marguerite and the whole cast unites against him.

Méphistophélès turns the wine to blood just to create problems and when Valentin challenges him to a duel his sword falls apart. The broken sword makes a fine cross and this defends Valentin, Siebel, Wagner and the rest of the chorus from further harm as they sing a proud male ensemble, with Siebel's female voice on top.

As the number closes, a waltz tune begins and the chorus (men and women) is back, dancing around. Faust and Méphistophélès talk as Siebel runs around looking for Marguerite. She finally appears and is introduced to Faust, who invites her to dance. In her brief two phrases of singing she declines and wends her way into the wings as the dance crescendos to a frantic climax and Act Two ends.

In Marguerite's garden, Siebel is lurking hoping to leave a gift of flowers. The problem is that Méphistophélès has cursed him and everything he touches wilts and dies. As he's still a young boy, this could cause huge problems. I love seeing a mezzo soprano sitting high on the fence with what might appear to be a parcel of fish and chips under her arm. We soon learn that it's not her lunch but the flowers, which keep dying. In this little aria Siebel overcomes the curse by washing his hands in holy water. He leaves his present and disappears. Faust, joined by Méphistophélès, enters and sings a most wonderful aria to the chaste place where Marguerite resides. It's a moment in the opera repertoire that, if it's done well, suspends time. I've had the pleasure of enjoying one or two really fine performances of this aria, but that's rare. Mostly the singer performing the title role saves his voice throughout the aria in readiness for the high C of the penultimate phrase, then misses it. This is when you just want to leave the building.

Méphistophélès leaves a casket of goodies for Marguerite near the posy from Siebel and the stage is cleared for the entrance of the prima donna.

Marguerite is one of life's lovely people but she's incredibly naïve. The meeting with Faust in the last act has left an impression on her and she idly moves around the stage singing a ditty called 'Chanson du Roi de Thulé' (the Song of the King of Thulé), interrupting herself to comment on her liking for Faust. Suddenly she sees Siebel's bouquet and within a second she discovers the casket left by Méphistophélès. As she opens it we hear a bright C major chord in the orchestra, topped by the tinkling of a triangle – this is an instrument that cuts through any volume – and she squeals with joy as she feasts her eyes on a pile of jewels. Isn't this a great cue to sing an aria? Not to disappoint, Gounod supplied her with a waltz song, 'L'Air des Bijoux' (The Jewel Song), where she tries on every bit of finery and fancies herself as a princess. To complement her folly, she sings a collection of trills and runs ending with a high B.

The last known castrato, Alessandro Moreschi, was the only member of that species to have made recordings. Even though he was not up there with the greatest we get a glimpse of the supernatural quality that the castrato voice held. There's a great story of Moreschi performing at a royal command performance for Queen Victoria. His aria selection included Marguerite's 'Jewel Song'. Queen Victoria must have had to hold back a chuckle as she watched this man in his 60s, with a full beard, looking at his reflection in the mirror and singing, in disbelief, 'It is not Marguerite. It is the daughter of a king!'

Now we meet Marguerite's minder Martha. She's the older woman, a mezzo soprano, and is needed to sing a quartet with Marguerite, Faust and Méphistophélès. Martha is delighted that Méphistophélès seems to have taken a shine to Marguerite. In actual fact he's enabling Faust and her to chat alone. They obviously love each other but Marguerite panics when things get too intimate and rushes away. To finish Act Three, Méphistophélès lures her back to Faust's embrace and they kiss as the devil laughs with fiendish glee.

My first *Faust*, actually the first complete opera I conducted, was directed by an Englishman famous for his acid tongue. At the drop of a hat he could make almost any cast member dissolve into tears, and did so with relish. But his production worked. It had been brought forward in period to the Victorian era, where the cultural opinions were parallel to those of the original plot. He added four scantily clad musclemen who lingered around the stage with Méphistophélès. They were his 'boys' and would magically appear at the click of a finger. In a rather ingenious manner, they were choreographed to perform the Jewel Song with Marguerite, although she could not see them. They presented Siebel's posy, opened the casket of jewels and, throughout the aria, hung more and more baubles on our soprano. At the end she was decorated like a lavish chandelier. As an opening night surprise for the Marguerite, I had myself photographed in one of their costumes but, somehow, it didn't look quite the same.

This is where things get messy in the plot and almost every production differs in the placement of scenes. I'm used to the following.

When Act Four begins we discover that Marguerite and Faust one night together had produced more than affection. Marguerite is pregnant and sorry that she's in this predicament. Siebel is with her and consoles her in a small boring aria. The sounds of returning soldiers cue the famous Soldiers' Chorus and we welcome the return of the disturbed brother Valentin. He's not in a good way, having heard about his sister, and he's ready to kill. He picks a fight with Faust but doesn't realise that Faust has the assistance of Méphistophélès. They sing at each other in an heroic trio, then fight as well as opera singers can. Valentin is fatally wounded, as Martha and the other town gossips enter along with Marguerite and Siebel. Before he snuffs it, Valentin curses his sister, then dies in true operatic fashion.

The scene changes to a church confessional. Marguerite has come to ask for forgiveness only to find Méphistophélès in the guise of the priest. Added to that problem, there's also an offstage (or sometimes onstage) chorus of demons plus a church organ that rattles the rafters. All in all, it's a marvellous scene with a great tune that Marguerite sings at the end. The most gripping coda to this part that I've seen had Méphistophélès, in clerical gown, holding Marguerite until she had a miscarriage. Quite effective in the theatre! That closes Act Four but, as there are only about 15 minutes left, it's usually a quick scene change.

Act Five is sometimes set in a prison with Marguerite jailed for murdering her child, or in a madhouse. Let's take the latter as it follows the reading of our tale so far. She's lost her sense of reason following the loss of Faust Jnr. Méphistophélès has brought Faust to see the result of his conquest and, eventually, to claim his payment. In a moment of recognition, Marguerite sings to Faust of the old days – or day – when they were in love. Like other masters of music theatre, Gounod recalls several of the tunes from previous pages in the score so the audience can reminisce on times gone by. Just when you suspect that all's well, Méphistophélès loudly demands his fee. He's come to take possession of Faust's eternal soul as in the terms of the signed contract in the opera's opening scene. This triggers off what might be the most uplifting trio in all opera. As Méphistophélès insistently calls for Faust's soul and Faust cries for help, Marguerite sings to the heavenly angels to assist her in her time of need. She collapses as Faust is dragged down to hell. To top it all off, this is followed by a chorus of offstage angels who wash all the sins away, rather as the Rhine does at the end of *Götterdämmerung*.

Gounod's *Faust* can be extremely moving and invigorating. Its score is riddled with melody. It has a great sense of operatic tradition, even in the face of the most ludicrous modern production values, and it survives in my Top 10 list. Take a friend and be ensnared by an operatic masterpiece.

RIGOLETTO

I'VE ALWAYS BELIEVED that Giuseppe Verdi's *Rigoletto* is the best work to initiate an opera virgin. It has not only a fabulous storyline but a score absolutely overflowing with melody and drama. What more could a newcomer ask for in a night out at the theatre?

The opera's story is simple. A sexual deviant aristocrat, the Duke of Mantua, has been enjoying a young girl, Gilda, who happens to be the daughter of his court jester, Rigoletto. The Duke doesn't realise that fact until two-thirds of the way through the opera. The father of the girl pays a hit man, Sparafucile, to kill his daughter's abductor. Unfortunately, love gets in the way and the daughter sacrifices her own life for that of her boyfriend. In the closing minutes of the opera, Rigoletto is presented with the body, only to discover that the merchandise is not what he paid for. It's that simple. The bad news is that there's no refund.

The opera opens with ominous repeated notes

on trumpets and trombones, the rather scary vendetta motif that signifies there'll be tears before bedtime. The strings join in, to heighten the pulse rate, and the percussion (timpani and cymbals) and woodwind accent the climactic moments of the heavy musical drama. The mood fades as quickly as it grew and we're left with those eerie trumpet notes. Before you know it, the tension builds again and we're back in the dramatics for a rather fiery end. Basically, the orchestra tells us what the final pages hold for the audience – rather like reading the last page of a murder mystery first.

The curtain rises, if you're lucky enough to have a traditional production, on a party held at the Duke of Mantua's palace. In updated productions, which are usually Mafioso or *film noir* based, it's set in a fabulous room in a gangster's mansion. Both ideas can work if you have a clever director. The chorus is dancing to band music heard from another room. Composers of this period liked to incorporate smaller orchestras or bands that play in areas of the theatre other than the orchestra pit. As I've explained, an offstage band has its own set of problems assembling, playing and synching with the production. Verdi made this one easy initially. After the prelude and as the curtain rises for Act One, only the offstage musicians are playing. They continue for several pages by themselves with only the television monitor to guide the assistant conductor or music staff person who is keeping them together.

As this slightly muted orchestral tune seeps from the wings, the idle gossip between the principal tenor, the Duke of Mantua, and his little offsider, Borsa (translated as Bag), is centered on their affection for the ladies. In fact, they're interested in anything in a skirt, as long as it's quick and doesn't involve committment. (Such an 'old fashioned' thought). A mere 16 bars before the Duke gets to sing his first aria, 'Questo e quella' (This one or that one), the pit orchestra joins in the performance. This stops the offstage band for a few pages.

The Duke's aria is a breezy little number in which he celebrates the disposable woman. Rather than ending on a tenorial high note, the play-out music slaps straight into a minuet. It's a simple, graceful dance and sung dialogue ensues between the Duke and the Countess Ceprano, whose husband is a nobleman in the Duke's court. Let this confirm that any woman is his prey. The verbal foreplay is interrupted by the arrival of the court jester, Rigoletto.

It takes a certain type of performer to portray this Hamlet of operatic characters. To make Rigoletto more human, Verdi and his librettist, Francesco Maria Piave, gave Rigoletto's difficult character a wonderfully sympathetic side, which we see a little later in the score. He is employed to entertain the guests with his wit. He's mildly good at this but tonight he will go one step too far. His humour is based solely on the difficult art of sarcasm. Oddly enough, he doesn't have too many friends. When Count Monterone, who is furious that the Duke has seduced his daughter, disrupts the party by announcing to the assembled crowd, in a resonant bass voice, that the Duke has sexually abducted his daughter, Rigoletto swings into action. This is his big moment to impress his current employer. In the most belittling way, he retells the events leading up to the rape. Oozing hatred, and supported by an immense outburst of volume from the orchestra, Monterone curses everyone ('la vendetta'), particularly pointing at Rigoletto. As the chorus sings of their horror in hushed tones, Rigoletto urgently feels the need to wash out his underpants. Left alone in an alleyway, our title character conveniently meets with Sparafucile, an assassin or hit man. In the most persuasive manner he convinces Rigoletto to trust him. The seed is sown!

Sparafucile is an important role and requires an artist of great vocal and physical presence to portray him with conviction. Unfortunately, he doesn't spend much time on stage or get a solo moment to sing an aria – or at least something resembling a tune – so he usually doesn't get too much applause at the end, as he should. His initial scene is a duet with Rigoletto. Verdi thrived on encounters between baritones and basses but they are rarely showstoppers. I conducted a one-off performance featuring three young singers who had participated in a high-profile national television competition. The winner performed the role of Sparafucile. He got through the scene without too much worry, but his applause was like something you'd encounter at a rock concert. The audience was obviously not made up of seasoned opera-goers and they reacted to the performance with a welcome honesty. In fact, when I came in for my Act Three bow someone called out 'Spunk' – and it wasn't my wife. My colleagues suspected that it was shouted by some visually impaired patron. Why do I suffer such treatment?

Left alone, Rigoletto contemplates his life, career and new-found killer contact. His constant misery is erased only by his love for his daughter. He flings open the door to his house as the music changes to a youthful, energetic tune that introduces us to the character of Gilda. In an extended duet – Verdi was particularly good at father/daughter duets – they discuss the matters of the day, their mutual affection and how much Gilda looks like her mother. All this is overheard by the maid Giovanna. (In opera, there's a maidservant even in the poorest of households.) Following a moment of distraction – an offstage noise that is actually the tenor sneaking into the house – they repeat a gorgeous tune combining their voices in reminiscing about Mrs Rigoletto. Rigoletto leaves the stage on the applause.

Now we get down to Gilda's story. Unbeknown to her father, Gilda has been seeing a cute guy whom she met in church - a really good place for pick-ups. He's been wearing Clark Kent glasses as a disguise so his identity as the Duke of Mantua remains a secret. Tonight he's bribed Giovanna to let him into the house for a quick rendezvous. Surprised at seeing her boyfriend, Gilda invites him to join her in a duet. More offstage noises are heard. This time it's the Duke's assistants, otherwise known as the gents chorus. Before the Duke races off, Gilda asks his name. Isn't it typical that they've spent so much time together and they don't get around to asking such particulars? He responds with the pseudonym, Gualtier Malde. Had he asked Gilda for her surname, trouble might have been avoided. The ensuing 'Addio' duet is self-explanatory.

Left alone, Gilda fantasises about 'Gualtier Malde', singing the famous aria, 'Caro nome' (Dearest name). This poignant moment, which shows us Gilda's naïve warmth, is also a renowned soprano showpiece. Rather than ending after the cadenza, Verdi carries the moment on, repeating the main tune as if in a dream. And Gilda is so caught up in that dream that she doesn't notice the entire gents chorus singing a sprightly, if soft, ensemble. They rush into the house and abduct her. The obviously vigorous music subsides as Rigoletto returns to find Gilda gone. He cries out – 'Ah, la maledizione!' (The curse!) – and the act ends.

Act Two opens with the the Duke of Mantua alone, singing a stylish aria about the purity of

Gilda and how bad he feels to have betrayed her. Borsa, Marullo, Ceprano and the courtiers race in and sing a rather jolly number, which could be mistaken for a 'soft shoe' melody, telling how they crept into Rigoletto's house and stole his mistress. In anticipation, the Duke sings a bouncy cabaletta, with high notes aplenty, and rushes straight to the awaiting bedroom. These few pages of the score are usually cut to save an endurance test for both tenor and audience. If it's a good night, the tenor will finish on a high D but good nights are rare.

The orchestra plays a slow limping motif that suggests both Rigoletto's emotional pain and his walking disability. (Did I mention that he's also a hunchback?) Although they don't really care, to his face the courtiers sympathise. 'Poor Rigoletto,' they sing. 'What's the news, jester?' He responds with a charming, 'Only that you are more of a bore than usual.' He's keen to keep on their good side. Throughout this conversation, Rigoletto searches for clues as to his daughter's whereabouts. A page (a soprano dressed as a boy) appears and chirps the news that a young escort has been seen with Ceprano. Obviously he's referring to Gilda. Rigoletto's emotions quickly build and burst as he informs the group on stage that they have, in fact, abducted his daughter. He sings the great dramatic aria, 'Cortigiani vil razza dannata' (Vile race of courtiers). At first the aria is a full-on bark for the baritone but it settles down as he pleads for the return of Gilda.

Naturally, Verdi made the most of this scene. The strings shower us with cascades of fury at the beginning of the aria, followed by the cor anglais and a solo cello joining the baritone at the aria's conclusion. Even a bad baritone can get good applause for this scene.

The assembled chorus members leave with their tails between their legs as a dishevelled Gilda runs from the bedroom door. She's no longer the virgin schoolgirl we loved in Act One. Now her hair is messed and she clutches a bed sheet to cover her naked body as she relates the story of the pick-up at mass by the handsome young tenor. Now she's cradled by her father's love. Performed by intelligent artists, this duet – another wonderful father/daughter collaboration by Verdi – can be the most moving of scenes in all opera.

In the background we see Monterone (remember him?) on his way to be executed for denouncing the Duke. Typical of his character, Monterone is riddled with hatred. Remembering his newest best friend Sparafucile, Rigoletto has the bright idea to avenge Monterone and organise for the Duke to be killed. With exultation he sings for revenge while Gilda pleads with him to forgive. Naturally they end on an extremely high note as the curtain descends on Act Three.

We have now arrived at the act that contains everything we consider to be 'operatic'. In a brief half-hour or so, we are presented with a super-famous aria followed by the greatest quartet in the repertoire. There's a storm, a trio, a stabbing and a death.

Act Four starts quietly with low strings. The mood lighting is dark but we can clearly see that we're in the red light district of Mantua where Sparafucile and his sister Maddalena are co-owners of a brothel. In fact it seems that Maddalena is the only girl working tonight and her only client is a regular, the Duke of Mantua. The orchestra starts the familiar oom-pah-pah accompaniment that reassures us that we're in three-four time and the Duke sings the ever popular 'La donna è mobile qual piuma al vento' (not 'the bird's got a bike' but better translated as 'women are as fickle as feathers in the wind'). It's the ideal thing to sing while you're sitting in a whorehouse.

Even someone who doesn't know opera knows this tune. As soon as the applause has died away, an energetic pulse in the orchestra begins as we are launched into the quartet. Actually, it is two duets performed simultaneously. The stage design has to have two clearly defined sections, outdoor and indoor. Inside we have the Duke chatting up Maddalena (why would you have to chat her up when she's already taken the money?) and outside we have Gilda with father in tow. Gilda can't believe her eyes when she sees the therapeutic massage that the Duke's giving Maddalena. At last she realises that she is not the only girl in Gualtier Malde's life. Rigoletto comforts Gilda while being intent on getting rid of the Duke. How this fits together musically is fascinating.

The quartet proper has the tenor wooing tonight's conquest 'Bella figlia dell'amore' (Beautiful daughter of love) for a whole two pages. Maddalena's response, a laughing melody to flirt with his advances, is capped by Gilda's emotional wailing on the other side of the stage. As it works out, Rigoletto's line is the least interesting and he never really gets to shine in this ensemble. One could describe it as a trio and backing baritone vocal. At any rate, if it ends on a loud high note, the ensemble rightly gains a big ovation and the story proceeds.

Rigoletto has bargained with the assassin Sparafucile, who is ready to murder his guest for a grand total of twenty scudi. (I have no idea of the value of a scudi – but it's sure to be slightly higher than a conductor's fee.) Rigoletto insists Gilda dress in men's clothes and flee to Verona. A thunderstorm approaches and the Duke quickly falls asleep, by himself, in a room upstairs. We know he's nodding off because he sings the 'La donna è mobile' tune to himself as he drifts off. The tune, and vocal performance, diminish as La-la Land approaches. Gilda returns, disguised as a man, and overhears Sparafucile promise that he will spare the life of the Duke if a suitable replacement can be found. As you'd expect, Gilda resolves to sacrifice herself for the Duke and enters the house, where she walks straight into

Sparafucile's knife. All this happens during the most noisy, thunderous storm. Backstage you have the male chorus making howling wind noises by singing chromatic phrases on a simple vowel up and down half a scale. It's dramatically effective but choristers hate having to wait in the theatre just to sing something in the wings. There's also the famous thunder sheet on which I became quite proficient in my younger days plus whatever the guys on the sound desk can play which relates to the sound of pouring rain. Somewhere in there, not totally disguised by the sound effects, is a brilliant melody along with some singing.

When the storm has passed, Rigoletto arrives with the money and is given a corpse wrapped in a bag. Just as he is about to throw the sack into the river, he hears the voice of the Duke singing that damn tune again. This is scored to be sung at the furthest distance offstage. There's a true story of a touring production that played smaller country towns. The cast, orchestra and crew had to make do with whatever conditions each local theatre offered. Some had little wing space, others none at all. At one performance, the tenor singing the Duke of Mantua suggested that, as the theatre had only a few feet either side of the stage, he would go outside into an adjoining field to sing his reprise of 'La donna è mobile'. Sounds like a good idea? The cast and crew were not aware of a lurking dog who was obviously guarding the property next door and thought the tenor was an intruder. The audience that night heard the following 'La donna è – *get off you mutt*' as the security patrol canine went about his job and wrapped his jaws around the tenor's ankle.

Back to the story. Our bewildered title character opens the bag revealing the body of his daughter. (He should have known something was different. The body of the Duke shouldn't have breasts.)There's another true story of an internationally famous soprano who needed to break wind while tied in the sack. She thought that the odour would have evaporated by the time the baritone opened it. She was wrong and both had a hard time hiding their mirth.

Because it's opera, Gilda revives for a few pages and declares she is glad to die for her beloved. She sings 'Lassu – in cielo' (In heaven above, near my mother, I shall pray for you evermore), which is one of the most meltingly beautiful melodies supported by heavenly flutes and shimmering violins. As she breathes her last, Rigoletto exclaims in horror, 'The curse!' as the curtain falls. This is opera at its best.

THE BASS

FEMALE SINGERS AND tenors can sound like your next door neighbour until you hear them vocalise. A bass commonly sounds as though he's singing an aria at you – in everyday speech. I suppose this continuous connection of the breath support to the vocal resonances is an easy way to practise. It keeps the voice 'in place'.

As a general rule, basses are tall and on the slender side. One American bass of the 1960s was nicknamed the 'singing milk bottle' (he never went in the sun either). After a few years, the tall and slender becomes the tall and portly. This is very handy for when one is singing the bass roles in the Rossini comedies. If Don Basilio in *Il Barbiere di Siviglia*, Mustafa in *L'Italiana in Algeri* and Don Magnifico in *La Cenerentola* are rotund, it helps with the buffoon characterisation. Good old Don Pasquale (in Donizetti's opera of the same name) is expected to be larger than life – in person and looks. A 'fat suit' undergarment in the opera company wardrobe is crafted as a moulded pillow that is strapped to the body before the costume is on. You can usually see the slight disappointment in the eyes of a chubby bass when the costume is large and he's not required to wear the 'fat suit'.

Other principal bass roles are more regal and authoritative in character. In their operas, Giuseppe Verdi and the composers of the bel canto era placed much emphasis on the importance of the basses, who tend to be fathers, priests, gods, demons or other extreme baddies. When it gets down to the nasty roles, they don't come much more villainous than Méphistophélès (in either Gounod's *Faust* or Arrigo Boito's *Mefistofele*), Cio Cio San's uncle in *Madama Butterfly* or the hired assassin Sparafucile in *Rigoletto*. There are the occasional bumbling fools: Falstaff (in both the Verdi and Otto Nicolai versions of Shakespeare's *Merry Wives of Windsor*), Baron Ochs (*Der Rosenkavalier*) and all those delightful charmers in the Gilbert and Sullivan string of operettas. Basses are a mainstay in the repertoire of Richard Wagner. If ever you're able to sit through a whole performance, you'd definitely realise that they're important characters.

Except for the small number of title characters delegated to the bass, most of their roles do not require the singer to 'carry the show' as would a soprano singing Madama Butterfly, a mezzo attempting Dalila or a baritone bellowing through Rigoletto. In the main, a bass gets one aria to show his stuff. On a good day, when he's playing the devil, he'll get two. A lot of the time basses are restricted to supporting the others in the cast and have only a line here and there. This may be why basses have a more relaxed, carefree attitude during times of other performers' intense stress. Many a time, when tempers and emotions rise in the rehearsal space, it's the bass in the cast who gives the reality check to the others. Out of nowhere you'll hear a deep voice announcing that we've spent too much time talking and not enough time rehearsing. Let's all have a break.

The natural and regular direction for a bass is to enter quite grandly, look physically impressive, sing his few lines with as much tone and volume as he can muster and exit, leaving the rest of the cast speechless. For him, that's basically a full day's work. He prefers to be scheduled to arrive at a rehearsal just in time to practise his stuff and then leave. He doesn't necessarily take an interest in the moves of his onstage colleagues.

When he is learning his music, in the privacy of a coaching room with a rèpètiteur, there is usually much more talking than singing. If the pianist is playing through an ensemble of, say, an opera by Verdi, the bass will sing only his solo lines. Never, *never,* will he sing if the chorus doubles his vocal line. Why should he bother to expel the energy when it's not going to be heard by the audience? (I've always thought that was a fair idea.) To reinforce this concept, several celebrity basses have retold the theory that, before drama was equally important to the singing in opera, the singers would move off stage if they weren't actually singing. This would happen even if their presence was vitally important to the story. To keep them on stage, Verdi and his compatriots wrote vocal lines (frequently the same as the chorus) so that the singer has to be in full view of the audience. Whether or not they actually sang these lines or simply mimed the text was entirely up to the individual.

A noted singer was renowned for his friendly basso – his wide vibrato waved at the audience across the orchestra pit – and for the fact that every performance he sang was billed as the 500th of that particular role. This was made even more curious when it was evident that, most of the time, he was still learning the music. He was generally content when he was centre stage holding forth, as many of the fatherly bass roles require. My first meeting with this character left an indelible mark on my memory. When we were introduced before a production rehearsal, he didn't greet me with the usual 'Hello' or 'Nice to meet you', as I expected. True to form, he immediately launched into his discovery of very large potatoes at the market that morning. As he described them, his mouth salivated in readiness for devouring the meal that night. This tall, portly bass, who had reportedly started his career as a tenor and eventually sang every principal male role in *La Bohème* (I never asked *how* he sang them), never attended late afternoon rehearsals no matter what the schedule required. It was some time before I was informed that he never missed the afternoon screening of *The Bugs Bunny Show* on television.

During a tour in the early 1970s, another celebrated bass found a massage studio in the local country town. Feeling in need of a gentle manipulation, he made an appointment and was attended to by a charming woman of Asian extraction. She had little command of the English language so the conversation was limited to a select few directions. Feeling quite comfortable during her attentive massage, the bass became sexually aroused by the positioning of her hands. She stopped and in her rather stilted English said 'You want wank?' After a second's thought he responded with a very resonant 'Yes'. The woman quickly disappeared behind an elaborately decorated screen and our basso waited for her next move. Minutes went by without a sign of her return. Just as he finally lost the hope of a happy ending and all his energy drained away, she came back with a smile and said, 'Good. You finished!' and they went on with the massage.

Fortunately these lovable characters still exist in the opera world. Recently we were rehearsing a new production of *La Bohème*. During a break in rehearsals the singers playing Rodolfo, Marcello, Schaunard and Colline, who were also longtime friends, were discussing the merits of a brilliantly musical colleague. In awe, the tenor was describing how this singer had a photographic memory. He could picture every page, every line and every note in his mind – and tell you where on the page it was. Our rather simple Colline, a bass who possesses a most attractive voice, beamed with enthusiasm: 'I can do that too. I just can't read it.'

THE MIKADO
AND OTHER OPERAS OF GILBERT AND SULLIVAN

LIKE ALMOST EVERY other musician brought up in English-speaking countries, some of my earliest performance memories are of the operettas of W.S. Gilbert and Arthur Sullivan. Even with the poorest amateur performance, the brilliance of this partnership shines like a beacon. Almost nothing can kill the audience's appreciation of the wit and frivolity of the lyrics of Gilbert and the simple lyricism of Sullivan's musical score. I have faint memories of my mother taking me to a performance of *Patience* at the local high school auditorium when I was still in primary school. I must have asked to go because there'd be no way that this repertoire would ever have interested my mother. The few things I remember about the performance are that it was accompanied on a pianoforte and that my kindergarten teacher, Mrs Woods, was one of the Twenty Lovesick Maidens – Lady Angela. For me, it was a surprise to hear her singing 'Go breaking heart' in the opening ensemble. Soon after that glowing moment I was asleep. However, I pored over the programme in the weeks and months following (I obviously had *no* life) and I was soon accessing LPs of the D'Oyly Carte recordings. That small seed soon blossomed into a forest and I was hooked on G&S. I sang all the principal songs and ensembles – to this day I never sing small roles – and even had the audacity to compete in the local Eisteddfod, performing the arias of Jack Point (*The Yeomen of the Guard*) and King Gama (*Princess Ida*). Soon the remnants of the original D'Oyly Carte Opera visited Sydney and I journeyed with the local pensioners group to attend what, even as a child, I could see were rather saggy performances of *The Mikado* and *HMS Pinafore*. They were the result of decades of the routine and the audience could see artists onstage having fun (even playing pranks) among themselves. I was furious, especially as I'd written to one of the 'stars' telling him of my admiration of his recorded work. I had been thrilled when he rang me at home one Sunday afternoon – my first contact with a 'famous' person.

Imagine how ecstatic I was to get the role of the Learned Judge in the high school production of *Trial by Jury*. I think that I probably nagged the teacher in charge so much that she gave it to me to shut me up. My performance was brilliant, as expected, and music historians will kick themselves that it wasn't documented on record for posterity.

A few years later I joined the Newcastle Gilbert

and Sullivan Players. It was my first time playing piano for real rehearsals. Little did I know that one had to follow a conductor's beat and interpretation, and collaborate musically with other colleagues in the orchestra. (Yes, it's a shame but I have to admit that we had a piano in the orchestra pit.) Initially, I rehearsed *The Pirates of Penzance*, then *Iolanthe*, and also sang in the chorus. *The Mikado* followed and I was back in the pit delighting in every amusing line and, of course, leading every musical cue from the piano – even though there was a conductor. A seriously scary moment happened during one of the matinées. Sitting there, obviously not concentrating on the production, I was fumbling through my score during some dialogue in Act Two to see what was coming up. Unfortunately I forgot where we were and, when the music cue came, instead of starting the sedate 'See how the Fates their gifts allot' quintet, I started playing the rather jaunty 'The flowers that bloom in the spring' trio. The orchestra obviously didn't follow my lead and for a few brief measures the audience thought they were listening to a score by Alban Berg. Very quickly I felt the firm hand of the conductor on my shoulder and she urged me to stop. After what seemed an eternity, we restarted the quintet. I wanted the pit to open up and swallow me whole. Many years later, when I was conducting this show in a professional production, I was pleased to discover that the quintet had been cut entirely.

Most people think that performing Gilbert and Sullivan is easy. Actually, it's as difficult to perform well as any other work for the opera stage. Misconceptions abound because G&S is sung in a familiar language and the music sounds simple. I have seen very few memorable performances. The worst happen when opera companies and performers think they are 'slumming it' in G&S. I have frequented *The Mikado* more times during my career than any other of the Gilbert and Sullivan operettas. In fact it was the score I was first contracted to rehearse when I joined the professional workforce. Australia has such a long history of performances of G&S that the national company has been nicknamed Operetta Australia – so regular are the revivals of these clever works.

A Canadian production of *The Gondoliers* that made a splash debut in the late 1980s boasted several things of merit. There's a big chorus that evolves into a flashy dance in Act Two called the Cachucha. The director's concept made it more effective by having each member of the ensemble bring on a stuffed fabric dummy as a dance partner. They were joined at the shoes and the stage suddenly looked very crowded. The Cachucha brought the house down every night, as it should. It was a brilliant idea.

In an Australian production of *The Gondoliers,* based on the Canadian version, we had to endure the quirky idea of casting the Duchess of Plaza Toro in drag. In the original production this character was played by a Shakespearian actor. We had a character tenor. Gossip was rife. It was not a particularly happy time for many of the cast members. The plot of *The Gondoliers* is as convoluted as every other Gilbertian plot. Marco and Giuseppe, twin brothers who are gondoliers, are believed to be heirs to the King of Italy – yes, both of them. Of course, neither is, but that's not the way these shows work. They are in love with Gianetta and Tessa. The show's opening number is quite long and introduces, in pseudo-operatic way, all the 'peasant' characters. It's quite long but not too boring. Following this, a boat appears carrying the regal party, the Plaza Toros. There's the Duke, the Duchess - preferably played by a woman – their daughter Casilda and the little drummer boy Luiz. (Need I tell you that, at the opera's finale, Luiz is named King? There, I've ruined it for you.) Added to this grand array of characters is a gypsy woman who makes a cameo appearance to name Luiz as… Her character is based on Verdi's Azucena in *Il Trovatore* except that she's a bit funnier. Ruiz, the gypsy woman, accidentally swaps the babies while in her care. All these things happen under the guiding hand of a Pygmalion figure called Don Alhambra, a Spanish dignitary who is the star of the show.

We had a director who was not really a director but a choreographer. In the rehearsal room he directed the production by referring to a video of the original Canadian concept production and transferring it to the cast on hand. There was no thought of change or even modification to feature our artists. One unfortunate moment came when the actor playing Luiz suggested interpolating some unique 'Australian' farm animal noises in his dialogue. The next day he had been replaced. In this business it is the quick or the dead. Complaints surfaced that I 'couldn't even play the Cachucha', a fairly simple, but seemingly endless dance in 3/8. It didn't take long for me to prove that I could play it (in every key possible – and, sometimes, several keys at the same time). This production has been resuscitated many times. Audiences seem to love it and they come in droves.

Every time you visit *The Mikado* it's a new experience. Like the libretto of Hugh Wheeler who wrote *A Little Night Music* with Stephen Sondheim, Gilbert's text for *The Mikado* is always fresh. Even though we can say every word along with the onstage performer, the lines sparkle anew at each hearing. Modern productions require contemporary additions and it takes real talent to write something that complements the bubble of Gilbert without seeming bland or lumpy. KoKo, the Lord High Executioner, has several opportunities to refer to contemporary matters. The best comedy is that which is fast and passes you by before you realise that it's happened. Remember the English school of vaudeville? In his cavatina – his entrance aria – KoKo lists a variety of people who are in line for the 'chippy chippy chopper'. Just like Don Giovanni, the great lover who never makes out with anyone during Mozart's opera, nobody is executed in *The Mikado*. (Shame really. I could list several dozen suitable victims.) KoKo mentions every political identity, showbiz celebrity, the latest fashion victim, the most annoying people known to the audience – and they love it. This type of comedy has been around since the birth of the art form. Sometimes, if the performer is adventurous, he will change the names from day to day, depending on the daily newspaper headlines.

This is all great fun unless you're the conductor trying to synchronise the stage and pit. There have been some very hairy moments in performance. Harder still is supplying a relaxed accompaniment to Yum Yum's Act Two aria, 'The sun whose rays', when she is terrified about when to come in. The aria is simplicity itself – a noted musicologist once said that it was the perfect blend of text and melody – and this, perhaps, is where the trouble starts. After a little flute tune the strings play three chords and then Yum Yum sings. The conductor clearly indicates each beat, one, two, three, then there's the biggest gesture to bring her in. Nine times out of ten she's wrong, but the audience would never know because the orchestra skips a beat – or adds one.

Pooh Bah is a pompous character who actually has the best role in the show. Sullivan wrote him as a baritone and it fits him well. KoKo is Lord High

Executioner and Pooh Bah is Lord High Everything Else. It's actually a role for a great singing actor. Added to his prestige, Pooh Bah is partial to bribery. Years ago I was connected to an 'updated' production devised by a dicey producer. The production toured and the performers had to fight for the standard, and legally required, touring allowances. After some loud backstage discussion, the onstage performance included a line spoken by Pooh Bah after looking at a measly bribe: 'What's this? Travel allowance?' The audience would not have appreciated the humour but the cast did.

The entrance of the title character is sometimes an impressive point in the show. He arrives with the rather sour Katisha, an unattractive woman who wishes to marry anything with a pulse. Katisha is the typical G&S contralto role. She's the unwanted who eventually ends up with someone (in this case it's KoKo). The Mikado is a bass and in the entrance scene sings a patter song describing his liking for executions. To 'make the punishment fit the crime' is his motto and he relishes every word. The chorus joins him in celebrating while he dances. In one production I conducted, the choreography had the Mikado moving downwards on a staircase one step per beat. In all rehearsals, and with each cast change (yes, there are two or three casts for each role) this went very smoothly if not exactly on the right beat. You must remember that singers are not dancers and generally have little sense of rhythm. The chorus was crouched at the foot of the staircase, bowed low. The inevitable occurred. We heard 'My object all sublime, I will achieve in tiiiiiiiiiiiiiiiime' and I looked up to see the bass falling the complete length of the staircase. Like a seasoned performer, or trouper, he didn't miss his next line 'To let the punishment fit the crime ...'. The chorus members, still prostrate, were laughing so much that their bodies were vibrating. As they moved up to sing their chorus all we could see were red faces with tears streaming down their cheeks. At the curtain call, the same performer included a fake fall to remind the audience who he was – as if they'd forgotten.

At the same set of curtain calls, which were also choreographed to curtain call music, I would start the orchestra with the desired tempo, then move out of the pit to appear for the onstage bow. (I never take bows in the pit!) As it was a long run for the season, two of the main singers would click their heels on their bow. Not to be outdone, it was the conductor who did the highest cabriole and received the loudest applause for doing so. For future reference, this type of curtain call bow can only be done with this particular repertoire.

Arthur Sullivan was himself a bundle of giggles. He left places for music quotes, quite like those employed by KoKo and the Mikado in their lyric updating. There's a great ensemble in Act Two, 'The criminal cried', where KoKo, Pooh Bah and Pitti Sing describe the fake execution of Nanki Poo. This is just before we learn that Nanki Poo is the heir apparent to the throne of Japan and also betrothed to Katisha. The three go into grisly detail on the beheading and the victim's severed head nodding three times. At this point Sullivan noted that the piccolo player should play a tune that the audience would recognise. It's a really quick moment that can go almost unnoticed by the audience unless they're alert. Sullivan suggested one of the tunes from *HMS Pinafore*, but we thought that the theme from a popular television series would do the trick. It did and went without a hitch until the last performance of the season. As always, waiting to enter the pit I heard the instrumentalists practising the 'hard bits'. I distinctly remember hearing the piccolo playing the popular TV tune over and over. When it came to the point in the score, I looked over to the piccolo. He was looking along the row of woodwinds to see the clarinettist placing a saxophone – an instrument not scheduled in the score but the instrument that plays the catchy *Simpsons* theme music – to his mouth. With a gleam in his eye, he played the loudest – yet most musical – television quote. Still the audience didn't react, but I did. If another performance had been scheduled, that orchestral member's name would have been on KoKo's little list, authorised by me!

NORMA

LET ME SAY from the outset that *Norma* is my favourite opera. It is also the opera that disappoints me most. I will explain.

Looking at the musical score it seems like a fairly simple, uncomplicated work. The storyline is not complex, though the characters are, and not too much happens dramatically to test your mind.

Vincenzo Bellini wrote for the greatest singing actors of his time, artists who were both fabulous actors and great communicators. Every nuance, every gesture, every bit of eyeliner was there to make an impact on the audience. The creator of the title role in 1831 was Giuditta Pasta. She had what they call 'it', something special in her performances that words cannot define but is sensed by the audience. Towards the end of her career, when her voice was in tatters from overstretching its natural abilities, a reviewer said that it reminded him of Leonardo da Vinci's *The Last Supper*: 'It's a wreck of a painting but that painting is the greatest in the world'. Obviously she was an extraordinarily gifted performer, that rare type of theatrical and vocal beast who is required to bring *Norma* to life. Without such a person, the opera is okay but not wonderful. In the hands of great interpreters, there is no better opera.

What's the problem? Well, the opera is filled with two things – incredibly beautiful melodies and long, drawn out recitatives. Singing melodies is one thing but supplying the emotional subtext for the drama is another. The term bel canto directly translates from the Italian as beautiful singing, but it means quite a lot more. Bel canto music requires the performer to inject emotion and drama into the melodic lines provided by the composer. Bellini, more than any other composer of this period, wrote simple phrases of extreme beauty, but without the addition of passion they are simply boring. In all this bel canto stuff there are tunes that make the score immediately accessible to the audience; it's up to the performer to convey the drama. Frequently the music suggests the opposite mood to the text and that's one of the great things that this repertoire gives to the artist – the opportunity to make theatrical choices. There is sub-text, joy of all great drama. 'Will I emphasise my regret for love of the tenor?' 'Will the loss of my children be the foremost idea here?' That's what a great artist would be thinking while singing these long, long melodious phrases, but all too often the singer is thinking, 'Am I going to get to the end of the phrase without having to steal another breath?' or 'Do I move over here later this scene?'

Bellini's extensive recitatives should not be problematic for a performer. It is documented that the composer would speak the text – the bits in between the arias and ensembles – at a natural pace until he was convinced that it was theatrically right. Only then would he put pen to paper. Following the composer's written directions, and with even a mild understanding of the character's emotions, the recitatives should be easy to deliver. Most of the time, this is not the case.

There's nothing worse than seeing singers, especially of the hefty variety, lumping around the stage wearing a toga and sandals. In the old days that's what everyone in this opera wore. Mind you, Norma usually had a crown worn with a fabulous wig and a toga/gown designed to give you the impression that she had a waistline. Even in modern productions, the costumes are still suggestive of the *Ben Hur* look, and I'm not just talking about the soprano and mezzo. With a few exceptions, the legendary Normas of last century looked quite acceptable in their Roman gear. Following the revival of the opera in the early 1950s heralded by Maria Callas – who eventually looked good in the costume – everyone wanted to sing the role. All the big bel canto specialists bought the score and had productions mounted especially for them: Leyla Gencer, Joan Sutherland,

Beverly Sills, Montserrat Caballé. These were all women who had a considerable history performing other roles and Norma was a peak, a role that their fans and critics assumed would display their talents and faults to the fullest. For the opera diva, Norma is Rose in *Gypsy*.

Let's give an outline of the story of the show.

Norma is a Druid high priestess who has vowed to remain celibate. Oddly enough, she has two darling children fathered by the Roman pro-consul, Pollione, which she's managed to keep secret for several years. One of the priestesses, Adalgisa, comes to confess to Norma that she is in love with a Roman guy called Pollione. This is where the merde hits the fan. He enters just as Norma is ready to vent her anger, which she does so violently that the Act One curtain comes down. Act Two starts with a melodramatic scene where we see Norma contemplating killing her children as they sleep. Because she's a lovely person, she can't bring herself to do the deed. Adalgisa interrupts for a cup of coffee and a chat. She has thought it through and decided she'll sever her ties with Pollione. All seems well until war is declared and Pollione is captured. Norma tells her father, Oroveso, and the attending chorus that she has been unfaithful and must be executed along with Pollione. The final scene sees them going to their death by immolation, with Adalgisa standing by as the adopted mother to the children.

I had seen *Norma* in performance a few times in

my teen years. Three Normas presented three quite different interpretations. In a rather terrible production from the 1970s, British soprano Rita Hunter was terrific. Although she was a very large woman, her face and heart were full of drama. She was famous for this role, along with her Brünnhilde and big Verdi roles. Her voice was big and penetrating though the quality was like a loud soubrette. Like a little girl. The audience didn't like her because of her size but I enjoyed this introduction to the work. Several years later I attended performances by Joan Sutherland along with one by her understudy. The understudy was more than proficient (I especially remember her wearing clear-heeled shoes that gave the impression that she walked on tip toe), but Sutherland virtually owned the role for many years. One of her Adalgisa colleagues told me that she stood in the wings at each performance in sheer admiration of Joan's Herculean ability to sing this long and arduous role with apparent ease. Her fullness of vocal tone and ability to ride those big orchestral surges were unmatched in her time, but for me it was her absolute musicianship and humanity that stood out.

My first association with a production of *Norma* came as rehearsal pianist and prompter. The soprano engaged to sing the title role had cancelled and her replacement for this production was the celebrated Bulgarian soprano Ghena Dimitrova. I remember her and her husband sitting in the rehearsal room looking like members of the KGB. She spoke almost no English and rarely smiled. Years of singing the biggest dramatic roles in the Italian soprano literature had taken their toll on the quality of her voice but she could still honk out the most remarkable sounds. She was a renowned interpreter of Norma but more famous for her Abigaille in *Nabucco*, as well as the title role in *Turandot* – huge sings that require loud voices. Ghena certainly had that in abundance. When she sang you could usually hear no one else. If you could, they sounded like mosquitoes beside her. The sheer force of Dimitrova's two high Cs just before the interval, where she discovers that Pollione is the new boyfriend of her maid, made my ears ache. One could imagine that sitting in the first few rows in the audience would be like being blown away by a cyclone.

On one occasion, Ghena came as my 'date' to a performance of a Mozart opera, but she insisted on leaving at the interval because 'They're all singing in falsetto!' Ghena used to vie for the title of loudest soprano in the world with the Hungarian Eva Marton. Recently when Marton did a series of George Gershwin concerts her opening number was *Yentl*'s 'Papa, Can You Hear Me?' Can they hear her? It's deafening. Not deafening enough, however, for me to point out that *Yentl* was not written by either George or Ira Gershwin.

Whether it was her lack of the language or the reticence of her culture, Ghena was not the usual chatty imported star. She was employed to sing Norma and sing it she did. There was not much else on offer. The new production was simple, perhaps a little routine, and she injected some of the required drama into the score. In fact, her declamation of the recitatives was fantastic. I was hooked on every word and she made it sound natural. Her supporting artists were less competent with both language and drama.

Ghena Dimitrova did all that was asked of her by the director but without much conviction. Her entrance at the rear of the stage was not spectacular. She declaimed the all important opening recitative profoundly – just as she'd learnt it years beforehand – then sang the loudest version of 'Casta diva' (Chaste goddess) that you'd ever need to hear. During the flute introduction, which plays the lingering melody for several bars, Ghena had been directed to hold Norma's sickle in various positions as part of the prayer process. Though she did the movements as choreographed, it still looked as if she was signalling directions to a plane on the tarmac. Each night I had to look away at that moment for my own sanity. Apparently as her voice grew louder so did my voice from the prompt box. Colleagues recall the volume of my 'Casta diva' at dinner parties.

The party following *Norma*'s opening night was a treat. The director of another production in the company's repertoire that season was known for his viper tongue in denouncing colleagues. His compliments on the *Norma* were all too few and he loudly stated that Adalgisa and Pollione met and sang their scene in front of what looked like a concrete toilet block. He had an acidic wit but he was correct on that particular matter.

As part of my staff duties, Ghena requested me to play piano for her vocal warm-ups before performances. It took enormous courage and calm to survive that aural ordeal in her small dressing room. She adored me and asked me to be her pseudo-nephew. My Italian was so poor and her English so limited that we never really managed to understand each other. I distinctly remember her fingers playing with the curls in my hair while she was warming up. Is that kinky?

Some years later I was in New York, having just married, and literally bumped into Ghena at the stage door of the Metropolitan Opera. She swept towards me and enveloped me in a full embrace. After suffocating in her cleavage for a moment, I came up for air. She looked at me with tears in her eyes and said, 'Briano. My husband ... dead!' (I understood that one) and we quickly organised a meal with my new wife in tow. The conversation was slight, but we spent the couple of hours nodding when she spoke, looking sad when tears welled in her eyes and laughing when she did. She did the same for us. It was a lovely, memorable and bizarre evening.

I will never forget my first experience of conducting this opera. The performance received great acclaim worldwide and many aspects of the production were excellent. As usual, my main objective was that the audience be taken on a musical and theatrical journey. The petite Russian soprano who performed the title role was articulate, sang well and emoted when she was singing by herself. Originally she had been asked to perform the lesser role of Adalgisa but she wanted the higher trophy. That was a good indication of the prima donna temperament needed for the title role. With some rejuggling, we cast her as Norma alongside a high soprano as Adalgisa. This upset a few diehards who insist that it should be sung by a mezzo voice. My explanation is that Adalgisa is the younger, sexier of the two girls. Why else would Pollione drop Norma and go with Adalgisa if she looked and sang like a truck driver? On paper this all looked good.

It took me little time to realise that Russian sopranos are a breed of their own. Our soprano did not sing at rehearsals nor did she ever communicate with her fellow artists. Duets became two soliloquies. She hated the costumes. She hated everything. Her list of complaints was longer than Don Giovanni's list of conquests.

Our trouble started when the director asked her to cut a branch of the sacred olive tree with her sickle. Actually a group of choristers held the branch and dropped the desired prop at a specific moment in the music. Our Norma couldn't (or wouldn't) lift her arm high enough to suggest the cut. We had a small prop ladder designed – in the style of our 19th century production – but she informed us that it was too high. The director showed his stepladder choreography several times to alleviate any fear. 'No, not possible,' and she reminded us that she was wearing heels. This was only the start of something that would grow out of all expectations. When it came to the stage rehearsals, she refused to carry the dagger that is intended to murder her two sleeping children. 'Is too heeveey,' was her complaint, delivered in a fake weak voice. After some vigorous discussion with the soprano during the tea break regarding the lightness of the dagger we started Act Two again. She came on with fire in her eyes, moved across the stage to where the sleeping children had been placed, raised the 'heeveey' dagger then, rather than dropping it as directed, threw it to the floor, where it bounced its plastic way across to the other side of the stage.

Frequently, artists conserve their voices and energies while rehearsing so they can concentrate on the 'acting'. As opening night speeds closer, the singers add more voice to build stamina. Arduous roles like that of Norma need a lot of vocal and physical stamina and we all wondered when our Russian diva was going to start pacing herself. So far she had not sung one note during the four weeks of rehearsal. More concerning was that the Pollione and Adalgisa had not balanced their voices with her in rehearsal. We had an understudy but she was also singing Clotilde, the maid. The dress rehearsal came and our diva decided that she'd save herself for the performance two nights away. Everyone really needed to hear what she'd offer, including the chorus and orchestra. A television crew came and asked if she'd sing the 'Casta diva' for the camera. She obliged but, as soon as that was over, she went mute, still doing the stage movements. We had an audience in the house. Strange as it might seem, I sang every other note of Norma's role while leading the orchestra – and received a decent ovation. Our Russian soprano sang every note at all paid performances.

You really have to be a diva to get the most out of this role. Back in the 1970s, a season of *Norma* was planned at the Royal Opera Covent Garden, starring the Spanish soprano Montserrat Caballé. For several years she'd made it her signature role and she was usually magnificent. At the initial ensemble music call, she and the glamorous American soprano (ex-mezzo) Grace Bumbry rehearsed their two great scenes together. Bumbry was scheduled to move up to the title role later in the season following Cabellé's departure. Norma has two extended scenes/duets with Adalgisa and traditionally they have been transposed down a whole step to make the role more comfortable for Norma. At the rehearsal they came to the line 'Nel Romano campo' (Take them to the Roman camp) which is the usual point for the modulation. Strangely it remained in key. Caballé stopped and asked why she had to sing, what was for her, a whole tone higher. It was explained that with Grace Bumbry singing Adalgisa and Norma in the one season, she had to keep her voice 'high'. Taking the duet down might make it uncomfortable later on. Caballé understood the difficult situation and tried to work the higher key into her voice. She managed a couple of performances then left her contract early from vocal exhaustion. Bumbry took over the title role and the English mezzo Josephine Veasey sang Adalgisa. When the score came to the pivotal 'Nel Romano campo', guess what happened? It was transposed down. That's power for you. Even later in the run, the other American soprano (ex-mezzo) Shirley Verrett claimed the role as her own. She was a great artist, singer and actor and gave Norma her all. Unfortunately, one can't be in control of the small things in life, and during a performance – in the scene where Norma strikes the sacred gong three times to assemble everyone on stage – the end of the prop striker, which no one realised was loose, fell off on the third strike, flew in the opposite direction and hit a non-singing actor, knocking him out cold.

THE BARBER
OF SEVILLE

FOR NEARLY TWO centuries *The Barber of Seville* has survived, despite constant musical and theatrical abuse. Let me state from the beginning that this brilliant comic opera – surely one of the greatest ever written – can be one of the dreariest and most embarrassing nights spent in the theatre. So far, I have worked on almost a dozen different productions of this popular opera, several of which have even endured eight or nine revivals. As a working musician I expect to see many more before I go to meet Rossini himself in his big kitchen in Heaven. (Rossini was well known for his culinary skills – indeed, it is said that he wrote his first hit tune, 'Di tanti palpiti', as he was waiting for the rice to boil.)

I need not retell the oft-told story of *The Barber of Seville*. Sure, it's the first part of the trilogy created by the French playwright Pierre de Beaumarchais and deals with the efforts of Count Almaviva to win the hand of Rosina, the ward of

Dr Bartolo. The Count Almaviva is assisted by the town's factotum, Figaro. Although he gets to sing the famous 'Largo al factotum' as his entrance aria, Figaro is not the star of the show. He might feel as though he's Pygmalion pulling the strings but it is the Count who does all the work. The other characters – Rosina, Dr Bartolo, Don Basilio (the singing teacher), Berta (the maid) and Ambrogio (the almost non-singing servant) – are merely characters who are manipulated by the Count, with the help of Figaro, in his quest for love.

Let's start with the overture. Many history books relate that Gioacchino Rossini crafted the score of *The Barber of Seville* (or *Il Barbiere di Siviglia*) in a matter of two weeks. That in itself is an achievement but several of the tunes, indeed the entire overture, are lifted from the composer's earlier works. This type of self-theft was common practice among composers at the time. Handel did it all the time and no one ever complained about recognising the tune. Of course, records and other forms of sound preservation had not been invented and it would be difficult even for a genius to remember a tune he'd heard only once several years beforehand. These days we can look in the local CD section of the library to hear the exact same music and orchestration as the overture to two earlier Rossini operas as well as a choral version of the lilting tune that Count Almaviva sings in the opera's opening scene. About 20 minutes into Act One we are presented with a famous tune sung by Rosina who informs us that, even though she seems like a good girl, she can also be a viper. That same melody was sung by Queen Elizabeth I in Rossini's 1815 *Elisabetta, Regina d'Inghilterra*. So much for crafting a melody to suit a character...

After the orchestra plays that very famous overture the curtain rises and we find ourselves outside the home of Dr Bartolo, a medical practitioner who sings with the voice of a bass baritone. We're underneath the window of his ward Rosina. The Count is in the first of his disguises as Lindoro. A group of men from the town – the male chorus – is assembled by his servant Fiorello, who frequently understudies the role of Figaro, and they accompany 'Lindoro' on mock instruments as he sings the opera's first major aria, with a guitar added in the pit to let us know that it's early morning and that he loves Rosina. There's no response from the window and the Count pays Fiorello and the townsfolk for their services.

No sooner do they exit than we hear from the wings the voice of Figaro about to make his flashy baritone entrance, which has become one of the most familiar opera pieces to the general public. Other than the 'Vincero!' ending of 'Nessun dorma' from Puccini's *Turandot*, the 'Figaro, Figaro!' is a catchphrase that immediately means opera. Even terrible performances of this aria receive big ovations. In the aria, Figaro tells us that he's the town hairdresser so he's known by everyone and he knows their business – and has their confidence. Next we have quite a long passage of recitative where we meet not only Rosina and Dr Bartolo but the personality (they have one) of the continuo player. There's some foreplay as Rosina deliberately drops a letter from her balcony, Dr Bartolo tries to locate it and Figaro and Almaviva (still disguised as Lindoro – except Figaro knows who he really is) read the letter's contents to the audience. Almaviva serenades Rosina with a cute little tune in two verses, accompanying himself on the guitar. Each chorus is echoed by Rosina from above. The window suddenly closes as she is singing the second response and we have a short page of recitative before tenor and baritone sing a great duet. Here they contrive the next disguise and attempt at entering the house of Dr Bartolo.

That's the end of the first section of Act One. There's a change of set and we find ourselves inside the house in the presence of Rosina, who sings the famous aria 'Una voce poco fa' (A little voice I heard just now), in which she recalls Lindoro's serenade and then tells us what she really feels. Producers can have a field day when casting this opera. First, we know that Rossini wrote the role of Rosina for a lower voiced female. This is evident in the full score because Berta, the maid, sits on the top line with Rosina singing the second line, suggesting that Berta is soprano and Rosina a mezzo (at least). The interesting thing is that any female singer with some fluidity in her voice – who can sing some fast scale passages or coloratura – can be cast as Rosina. Although it was written for a middle range singer, the vocal lines can be tailored to suit any voice. Personal preference has to run second to who is the personality performer of the moment. If you're a tweety bird fancier, you can be beguiled by a trapeze-walking, high staccato soprano in the role. Perhaps Cesare Sterbini, the librettist, would have admired a more womanly, sensual mezzo-voiced performer to render that aspect of Rosina's character. That almost dodo-like rarity, the contralto, is a real curiosity. If you have the chance to hear such a singer in the role, it's worth the price of the ticket. That full-bodied round tone with a chest register that sounds almost like a tenor can be a religious awakening.

No matter who is cast, the conductor, or the coach, is expected to make Rossini's music fit her particular voice. That is what vocal ornamentation is all about. It should enhance the music to flaunt the virtues of the individual singer. If you have a great high E, well, the audience should hear it as regularly as good taste allows. An easy and clear trill on an F should also be on display because only a very skilled few have such a marvel. Singers have 'money notes' – sung pitches when the producers claim they can hear the ring of cash registers – which can be at either end of the range. You might note a celebrity mezzo singing up to a high B at the end of an aria then jumping down to the B two octaves below before finishing the phrase. Audiences love such crazy, dare-devil feats of terror. These types of singers are like vocal acrobats and the more they face certain death and win, the greater the applause.

The slimy Don Basilio visits Dr Bartolo. Basilio, the opera's bass, is usually costumed in a shabby, torn cassock with over-the-top make-up. Designers like to add a nose extension as well as several moles on his face. A grey untidy wig frequently finishes off the look. The main thing for us is that he has a fantastically sonorous bass voice to sing his 'La calunnia' aria. 'Start a rumour,' he suggests to the easily gullible Dr Bartolo, whom he has told of his concern that Count Almaviva is courting Rosina. This is a great aria, which gives the performer many interpretative options. As the orchestra plays a repetitive motif Basilio can colour his vocal sound to mimic the text. Enough is never enough. He has only one solo in this opera and really needs to make the most of every moment. The phrase 'less is more' does not apply to Don Basilio. I have vivid memories of a production in which a porcelain penguin exploded atop an onstage piano at a climactic point in the aria. I also had to try to remember to cover my ears as the bass drum came to prominence in the orchestra pit at the same point in the score: the continuo is sometimes seated near the percussion section. Basilio exits on a high note and we get on with the story. Figaro and Rosina chat. She knows that Lindoro has his eye on her and Figaro suggests that she write a letter to him. Of course, she's already written it and has it in her bra for safekeeping. She reaches in and presents the warm envelope to Figaro. The audience laughs – I've never understood why: it's such an obvious thing – and they finish the duet, the tune of which was also written for an earlier opera.

Next follows a very great aria for a very great performer. Might I add that, of all the characters in *The Barber of Seville*, Dr Bartolo is the one with the audience on his side. He's most deceived by the others and clearly gets the sympathy vote. I love the character. He is charming, can be very funny and has many dramatic opportunities. He commands every scene in which he appears. What more can a performer wish for? Bartolo was a prized role for baritones of the old school and he's best played by an artist of great experience. Bartolo's aria is pompous, tuneful and finishes with a *very* fast patter section riddled with tongue-twisting lyrics. It really is a bravura aria of the best kind.

Berta complains about the madness in the house and sneezes. I purposely omitted telling you about the very unfunny scene just after Rosina's 'Una voce poco fa' where Berta and Ambrogio, the other servant, sneeze and yawn their way through a page of recitative. She hears a knock at the door, sneezes again (more humour) and invites Almaviva, in his new disguise, into the house. Here begins the Act One Finale.

The finales to Rossini opera acts are very important, and tailored to perfection. Their dramatic shape and musical form are obviously the work of a master craftsman. The composer has created a theatrical journey in music starting with a clumsy march figure in the orchestra. Almaviva is now disguised as a drunken soldier and stumbles around the set calling out for Dr Bartolo. After he arrives, the ensemble builds with the addition of Rosina, Berta and Don Basilio. The musical temperature rises with the onstage confusion and peaks with the appearance of Figaro, who apparently comes to save the day. Within two minutes there's a really loud knock at the door and the male chorus sings an unaccompanied offstage announcement that they are 'the police'. When they appear on stage, there's even more confusion among the characters and some gabbled explanations from each of the principals. An officer, who is the chorister who won that cameo role, delivers his six-bar solo and is about to arrest them all. Almaviva, still as the drunken soldier, shows him an 'official' letter and everyone is silenced. Here we experience the wonders of Rossini's hushed ensembles. Almost whispering, Rosina slowly, and with silent pauses between syllables, tells us that she is frozen with fright and fear. In the same vein Almaviva, Bartolo, Basilio and Berta, join in, while Figaro vocally dances around them. Suddenly, usually with a loud sneeze from Bartolo, everyone comes to life again and they sing the final fast section that closes the act.

During my professional life, I have been in the pit for performances of *The Barber of Seville* as conductor, continuo player (fortepiano and harpsichord) and rehearsal pianist – more involvement than in any other opera. Working with repertory companies, one sees the standard works of Mozart, Rossini, Verdi and Puccini more than other composers.

The job of the continuo player is to support the recitative with the written chord progressions, and to enhance whatever is happening on stage by adding improvised musical comments. Conductors will have their preference as to what instrument is used for continuo. Standard practice is either harpsichord or fortepiano, which is preferable for this period of opera, but for almost a century, a normal piano was used because harpsichords were out of fashion. Mozart also suffered the indignity of this 'modern' instrument. Perhaps it's just luck that I've only had the more suitable keyboard instruments to play for myself and other conductors. Long before I knew anything about the art of continuo playing – some in this bitchy business might add that I still know nothing – I would try to create on the keyboard the magic that I imagined was being created on stage. Little did I realise that, with a few serious considerations, that's exactly what is meant to happen. With the speed of the way you play a chord, upwards or downwards, you can create a musical atmosphere for the drama.

Act Two of *The Barber of Seville* opens with Dr Bartolo alone, contemplating his fate. The score asks only for a single chord. In a standard production, he may be sitting alone in a comfortable chair as the curtain rises. A slow, ponderous breaking of the chord into separate notes might suggest that he's been there for ages. A recent production required a bit of stage action before Dr Bartolo sang. That gave me the chance to musically mirror in melodramatic fashion Dr Bartolo walking down the stairs of his surgery, greeting a patient, checking his notes, shaking the thermometer and placing it in the patient's mouth – all before we arrived at the B major chord which starts the scene. Some early training in playing silent film music finally had its rewards.

There have been times, and these return whenever I get really bored, when I've added extra ditties to fill out the chord structures. These clever tunes are improvised without rehearsal, so the additions might be catastrophic, unless you're really good. They should, in some cryptic way, comment on the action. My naughty additions have included everything from television themes, tunes from Broadway musicals, a whimsical combination of the staccato tune from the overture mixed with a favourite Abba song and quotes from operas of the same and other periods, as long as they are instantly recognisable. In fact, at one point audiences would leave requests at the stage door before the show and it was my goal to include every one in that performance. At times, the final few minutes of recitative seemed like a continuo concerto going on while the cast onstage went about with the rehearsed recitative. It was brilliant, but very naughty! One season, I made a list of all the quotes that had been added and it totalled over 200 during the run of a dozen shows. You can imagine how constricted I felt when another conductor wanted it played straight. At the break in the first day's ensemble rehearsal, he followed me into the music staffroom and quietly said, 'We cannot work together'. I had to be honest and my reply of 'Yes. I know!' did not win his affection. Fortunately, I was quickly switched to another opera running simultaneously.

Sterbini wrote endless pages of recitative in his libretto. It is not compulsory and it is generally accepted that a director will make suitable cuts to trim the storyline to the design of the production. Hence, every production of this opera will be different. That makes it hard for the singers too. There is a whole group of singers who specialise in their particular roles in *The Barber of Seville*. They tour the world from one production to the next but, each time, they have to learn, delete or rewrite bits of that joining dialogue, and this can cause havoc in performances. As you know, and with opera singers it's even more pronounced, the first way you learn something generally stays with you, no matter what. I've been in the pit playing the accompanying harpsichord when a singer, for no apparent reason, suddenly goes off on a tangent, singing another whole page of dialogue, or omits half a page merely because he or she can't remember which production they are doing. If you think that this calls for the utmost inventive skill from the harpsichord player, to save the singer from embarrassment, try imagining what it would be like to be onstage.

Getting back to Act Two... That brilliant thespian Count Almaviva has now re-entered the house, this time disguised as Don Alonso, Professor of Music and a pupil of Don Basilio. The master is sick so he, Don Alonso, has come to give Rosina her singing lesson. Of course, Rosina sees through the disguise.

Since the opera's premiere, the lesson scene in Act Two has been a free-for-all opportunity for each Rosina to strut her stuff. In the original score, Rossini wrote an aria, 'Contro il cor' (Against a heart that invites love), a rather mild piece about love always being victorious. The vocal demands are not too tricky, unless the singer has little technique, and it has a few scales and arpeggios scattered throughout its four-minute duration. Because he was writing for a specific theatrical moment of comedy, Rossini added a few interjections from Count Almaviva/Don Alonso along the lines of 'Don't worry. I'll save you from this boring life'.

When this original aria is used in a production, Dr Bartolo usually sits nearby to observe the 'lesson' but promptly goes to sleep, only to wake up at the two climactic moments of passion between Rosina and the tenor. The loud snoring and overacted waking up can sometimes amuse the audience.

Throughout the history of this opera, sopranos, mezzos and contraltos have replaced Rossini's 'Contro il cor' with a number – or numbers – of their choice. In modern times, taste has confined the repertoire to being, at least, an aria written by Rossini. It might be from an opera they would like to add to their repertoire like *L'Italiana in Algeri* or *La Donna del Lago*, both very popular repertoire pieces in the 1970s and 1980s. Going back a few generations, 'Bel raggio lusinghier' (Bright ray of light) from the same composer's *Semiramide* might be performed. These changes to Rossini's score happened even in reputable theatres like the Metropolitan Opera in New York. In the 1950s and 1960s, if a high soprano were cast, she might be obliged to sing one of the following: the set of variations by Heinrich Proch, 'Deh, torna mio bene' (a fairly standard supplement), the 'Twinkle Twinkle Little Star' variations by Adolphe Adam (also a common replacement), 'Lo, Here the Gentle Lark', Luigi Arditi's Parla Waltz or his 'Il Bacio' or any number of other parlour songs. Early last century, the divas of the Golden Age would perform anything they wanted as long as the final item was 'Home, Sweet Home', sung to their own piano accompaniment. Perhaps the most bizarre documented lesson scene was that performed at the Polish soprano Marcella Sembrich's farewell in 1906. She sang the sleepwalking scene from Bellini's *La Sonnambula*, played a movement from the Mendelssohn Violin Concerto (she was also a concert violinist), continued with Johann Strauss's 'Voices of Spring', Chopin's song 'The Wish', a few other ditties, then rounded the scene off with 'Home, Sweet Home' before going on with the rest of *The Barber of Seville*. What time did the audience get home that night?

After Rosina has received the total adulation of the audience, Dr Bartolo wakes up, applauds and offers his own little aria in the style of the greats of his youth. His idol was Caffariello, who was a famous castrato but Bartolo sings in his full baritone voice. His self-indulgent vocalising is stopped by the appearance of Figaro, who causes chaos on the set and manages to break a whole collection of Bartolo's finest china. Without much ado, Don Basilio arrives ready to give the singing lesson, and it's perfect timing for a quintet. The cast manages to persuade Basilio that he is actually ill, indeed that he has scarlet fever, and sends him off with a charming 'Buona sera' melody. Rossini, or perhaps Sterbini, wrote a false ending because Basilio makes an unexpected re-entry before being encouraged to leave for good. Figaro then starts shaving Dr Bartolo and we see him for the first time as the barber of Seville.

While the strings in the orchestra busy themselves with repeated notes galore, which are awful to play on the piano, we have Bartolo and Figaro on one side of the stage and the lovebirds on the other. Almaviva and Rosina waste no time in getting down to planning their elopement. Because the stage is small, and because we need some excitement at this time in the show, Bartolo overhears their conversation and orders Almaviva out of the house. This rather excited bit of ensemble tends to come adrift musically if either stage or pit decides to proceed at different tempi.

Left with the stage bare, that boring Berta (remember her?) comes on to complain about being a maid. At the end of her aria, the audience is encouraged to wake up so they can endure the *temporale* or storm. Several Rossini operas contain musical storms, which usually happen two-thirds of the way through the second act. Yes, they sound like a storm, only in music. Rossini writes the drip, drop sprinkle of the first raindrops for the flute. They are joined by other instruments as the drops become angrier until the full force of the orchestra blazes away for the peak of the storm. The storm dies down and we're left with Figaro and the Count Almaviva climbing a ladder to meet Rosina for the elopement. They sing a trio and tiptoe on their way singing the suitably tiptoe 'Zitti zitti, piano, piano' ('Softly, softly, and in silence'). As the ladder has been removed, they find themselves caught with nowhere to go. Basilio arrives with a notary (isn't that lucky?). The notary is a non-singing role but he is a good ham-actor and we see him marry Almaviva and Rosina. Dr Bartolo arrives a second too late and ends up having to be coupled with his housemaid. That sounds very Gilbert & Sullivan, doesn't it? Actually, I have no idea who Dr Bartolo ends up with. I added that idea for those directors among you who draw a blank at that moment in the score.

The Barber of Seville was not just an ensemble piece at its premiere, but a real showcase for the tenor singing Count Almaviva. For over a century it evolved into being a showcase for a soprano or mezzo soprano but it's easy to see that the original intention was to present the tenor as the central comic hero. He is seen in three disguises and in full regal splendour at the opera's conclusion. Indeed, Rossini and Sterbini gave him the 11 o'clock number, the star spot in the score. That scene contains what used to be considered a fiendishly difficult aria for the tenor – an heroic recitative followed by a tender aria and brilliant cabaletta (or lively finale), resplendent with energetic coloratura. And all this was supported by a backing chorus. Then the opera dribbled on to a pleasant finale with everyone singing how happy they are. But it surely was the tenor's show. During the years when the women grabbed every opportunity to show off and claim the show as their own, conductors and producers would simply cut that brilliant tenor scene, and the audience never knew what they missed. Every now and then from the 1960s onwards, a tenor would pluck up the courage to reinstate the scene but, by that time, singers had become less adept at the technically difficult Almaviva role. One could say that they were a tad boring. In the 1980s came a small handful of tenors, particularly those bred and trained in the Americas, who had the vocal ability, the theatrical spunk and the star power to once again make *The Barber of Seville* a vehicle for the tenor. Thanks to the superman efforts of Rockwell (aka Rocky) Blake 20 years ago, a few of the tenor superstars are now the publicity drawcards in this repertoire.

At first glance Rossini's score may look and sound like easy formula music, but it takes a great cast and conductor to give it the consistency and lightness of the best soufflé. Probably because the opera is based on the Beaumarchais comedy, it requires that fast French subtlety in the musical delivery. Unfortunately, endless productions of this wonderful score are hampered by heavy-handed readings from the conductor and director. If you're fortunate, the performance will lift you up and carry you away without ever suggesting that time has passed or that the music is fast, tricky and difficult.

In my opinion, placing an opera singer in a comedy without the addition of a very strong director and conductor spells disaster. There's nothing worse than a performer with good vocal ability and not much else trying to be funny onstage. We've all seen it, and it makes us cringe. I've always believed that the stage action must complement the flavour of the musical score. Audiences don't accept it from theatre or ballet companies yet, in opera, it seems okay to play the fool if it's comedy. I think it was the greatly respected actor Edmund Gwenn who said, 'Dying is easy. Comedy is difficult.'

TURANDOT

IF YOU CAN'T make a financial success out of Puccini's *Turandot*, you've got real problems. Every production that I've witnessed, whether on the podium, as part of the show or as a spectator, always wins the approval of the audience, owing to the sensational thrill of Puccini's music, coupled with the visual spectacle. Of course, it also includes the 'New York, New York' of the operatic repertoire – the tenor aria 'Nessun dorma'.

Many academics claim that *Turandot* is a flawed work because Puccini died before he was able to complete the final scene. It is true that, at the time of his death in 1924, he left only a few brief musical sketches of musical ideas for what was to be the great duet between Turandot and the Unknown Prince. In his wisdom, the conductor of the world premiere, Arturo Toscanini, commissioned the composer Franco Alfano, who was certainly not 'just a student' as some history books state, to structure an ending incorporating Puccini's sketches as well as his own ideas. The result is rather fantastic. Toscanini, however, decided Alfano's elaborate finale was too long and put a big red pencil through the sections he thought unnecessary – about two-thirds of the manuscript – leaving us with the finale we know today. In the late 1970s, productions around the world began to use the full Alfano ending, which really makes a grand impact as the score and drama erupt with dozens of offstage trumpets, choruses and an extra 12 minutes of music. In recent years, a number of respected composers have substituted their own final scene, but I much prefer the 20 minutes of showbiz that Alfano supplied.

It is commonly known that the world premiere performance stopped after the death of Liù, the slave girl, and Toscanini turned to the audience and said, 'At this moment the maestro put down his pen'. As Liù is the sympathetic character in the opera, I'm sure that she received a huge ovation that night.

Any *Turandot* production is usually gigantic in size and requires a gigantic number of choristers to fill out the stage. Puccini was not generally known as a choral composer – one celebrity conductor told me he never conducted the score because there were too many choruses – but the score contains some splendid numbers, particularly in Act One. That act allows the ladies' and gents' chorus to scream out the opening wails, sing the vigorous executioner music, wallow in the 'Moon Chorus', feel sorry for the Prince of Persia (whose only duty is to cross the stage in preparation for his execution. A chorister sings his 'Turandot!' from the wings a few bars later) and to pick up from Calaf's first big aria at the act's conclusion. After that, the rest of the chorus music lets us know when something interesting is going to happen.

The opera opens with some swift orchestral phrases that have an oriental flavour – this is Puccini letting us know that we're in China. It could also suggest a knife severing a head, so sharp is the musical intent. We're immediately introduced to the Mandarin, the game show host who tells us the rules of the game – whoever can correctly solve Princess Turandot's three riddles will win her hand in marriage. One wrong answer will result in decapitation.

The bloodthirsty chorus cries to bring on the executioner so they can witness the death of the most recent failure, the Prince of Persia. They then go feral as the guards push them away and Liù (the slave girl), Timur (the dethroned King of Tartary) and his son Calaf appear. They're on the run from the invaders. Timur is old and blind and Liù is guiding his way. Why? Easy answer: because she's in love with Calaf. One day in the palace Calaf smiled at her and now she's an operatic stalker.

Soon there's a dance of the executioner's assistants. In most productions, all you can see at this moment are the glistening blades of their weapons as well as the heavily oiled abs and six packs of musclemen, employed by the director as eye candy. Rehearsing these non-singing, non-actors can be an endurance test for all concerned. The combined IQ of six musclemen is a two-digit figure and their sense of musical rhythm, at the best of times, is vague. When the assistant director – because the main director would never lower himself to work with this species of performer – rehearses them, they speak in single syllables and shout repeatedly, 'One, two, three, now! One, two, three, now!'

At the peak of this mass hysteria, those opening sharp chords are reheard and the chorus gazes out into the auditorium and sings to the moon. In the wings, children's voices sing the plaintive tune that we will come to associate with the character of Turandot and the funeral cortège of the Prince of Persia, who is still alive, wanders across the stage. The procession stops only long enough for the figure of Turandot to be seen giving the commanding gesture to the executioner. Actually, Turandot doesn't sing anything at all in Act One, or for the first half of Act Two. From then on, it's a yell a minute.

The voice of Turandot is not one that requires beauty, although it should. Many sopranos have come to grief singing the role because they scream it as loudly as possible, frequently with a wobble wide enough to accommodate several trucks. At full throttle, hearing one of these Turandots can be an unsettling experience. Just because the great

Swedish soprano Birgit Nilsson sang with a beacon-like volume doesn't mean that all who follow her should emulate those decibels. (I once heard a receptionist, new to the job on the desk at an opera company, innocently ask, 'What's that sound like a slaughtered pig?' I didn't have the nerve to explain that it was our new Turandot warming up.) A great Turandot, no matter how icy the character, should be liked by the audience. They should warm to her so that the eventual melting kiss in Act Three is the pivotal moment in the action. Audiences like to like the people on stage.

Because it's opera, Calaf becomes infatuated after just a single sighting of Turandot – 'My very soul has been embalmed by her fragrance!' (that's a direct quote from a singing translation). He decides to risk his head and enter the competition.

Now we get to meet three of the most boring characters in the operatic repertoire. They are comprimario, or character singers, who always appear together. With the given names of Ping, Pang and Pong, they feel safer sticking together. Ping is a full-on dramatic baritone and the other two are usually cast as nasal tenors. They are ministers in the court and are employed to deliver the conditions of entry for the Turandot competition. Calaf hears but does not listen, and confirms his entry as tonight's competitor Liù, pleads with him not to gamble away his life. His vision-impaired father, Timur, will lose his son and Liù will 'lose the shadow of a smile'. The end of this beautifully poised aria, 'Signore, ascolta' (My lord, hear me) is the first chance the audience gets to applaud. Liù is a sympathetic, hometown girl and if she delivers the final phrase absolutely pianissimo – as she should – the applause is guaranteed. Calaf then sings his first aria. In less than positive phrases he tells Liù not to weep. She might be Timur's only aid if he gets the answers wrong. As he throws out his climactic phrase, Timur, Liù, Ping, Pang, Pong and the chorus sing of their differing plights as Calaf strikes the gong. He sings the name of Turandot thrice to signal his application as the curtain swiftly falls on Act One.

Before the story has the opportunity to proceed, there's an extended scene where we get to know more about Ping, Pang and Pong. Do we care? The score itself contains a wealth of good music but, theatrically, these six minutes test even the most inventive of directors. Rarely have I known an audience not to be bored by this scene. An offstage band is heard, signalling the procession of the chorus, dancers and the arrival of a new piece of scenery – the square in front of the palace.

There's a great story concerning the design of this particular scene for a production in the 1960s, when the *Turandot* revival got into gear. The designer wanted banners hanging either side of a central staircase that was the focus of the stage design. As he had little or no knowledge of Chinese, he asked advice. The banners looked impressive with their 'authentic' ancient Chinese script. It was only after opening night that some audience members alerted him to the trick that had been played. The banners read, in modern Chinese, 'Eat at Joe's Restaurant', the workplace of the designer's adviser.

When all are assembled the Emperor Altoum, Turandot's father, enters to the chorus singing 'May our emperor live for ten thousand years'. He sounds even older in his ensuing crackly conversation with Calaf. Sometimes a very famous tenor in his much later years performs this cameo role. Good old Giovanni Martinelli performed it in his 80s several decades after singing the role of Calaf with great success. In 1938 he was cast as Calaf opposite the grand dame of English dramatic sopranos, Eva Turner. Excerpts from that season at the Royal Opera House Covent Garden were recorded and released commercially. The old emperor in that cast owned the fabulous name of Ottava Due, which translates as Two Octaves. Altoum is like the town shrink. He is there to make sure that Calaf knows what he's getting himself into. As when negotiating a performance fee, Calaf will not budge and Altoum agrees to the competition.

That annoying Mandarin makes a brief reappearance stating the rules of entry just in case we've forgotten, and Princess Turandot enters, preceded by the children's chorus. At last we get to hear what she sounds like. In a famous narration she tells the tale of her ancestor Lou-Ling who was dragged away and her voice silenced. It's not made clear if Lou-Ling was abducted, raped or killed. In any case, it's really screwed with Turandot's head and it's left her frigid.

This aria, 'In questa Reggia' (In this palace) is six minutes of declamation, ending in a rather passionate outburst of the emotions we hope to see her deliver at the end of the show. When Turandot proclaims, 'Gli enigmi sono tre, la morte una!' (The riddles are three, and death is one!) Calaf interjects one step higher in pitch: 'No, no! Gli enigmi sono tre, una è la vita!' (No, no! The riddles are three and life is one!). Then they sing the same phrase another step higher climaxing with a sustained high C in both voices. At best, it is a thrilling moment of vocal stamina as soprano and tenor try to outsing each other. Puccini knew what he was doing. I feel a touch of excitement even as I write.

When all is calm, the riddles begin. Turandot has been studying the Sunday cryptic in the *New York Times* and her questions reflect the best of that riddler. Puccini's librettists Giuseppe Adami and Renato Simoni excel in the theatrical build-up of tension as Calaf deciphers the clues. He almost faults on question two. Old Emperor Altuom lends moral support, the bloodthirsty chorus reminds him that he could die – Liù calls out 'Your love is at stake! (it's the only thing she sings in the whole of Act Two) – and, after a moment of slight hesitation, he manages to answer correctly.

Turandot is on edge as she presents the final

question. Rather stupidly, the questions are very self-centred and Calaf rejoices in his final, correct, answer, 'Turandot!' There's a swell of jubilation from everyone onstage except our title character. She pleads with her father but is twice advised that 'The oath is sacred'.

One celebrated production had the Turandot appear on a high platform, wheeled in by the dancers. She sang her aria and asked the riddles from high atop this contraption. After the third correct answer from the tenor, she moved down, stepping on the backs of the dancers, to stage level to plead with her father. At a school performance of this, the soprano was short and chubby and the audience of students tittered for the rest of the act.

So that we get to have an Act Three, Calaf responds to Turandot's negativity with a personal challenge. 'You gave me three riddles. I will set you one. If you can tell me my name, I will die at sunrise.' With that kind offer, the chorus again sings the praises of Emperor Altoum, and that ends Act Two.

My many seasons as a prompt for *Turandot* came in handy for my first season conducting the opera. The production was done without the aid of a prompt and, at the final performance, the soprano performing the title role was overcome with nerves and managed to forget the entire role in Act Two. I gave her the usual three or four words that began each sung phrase. She delivered those and made up the rest. This made the riddle scene even more riveting for the audience. They heard the conductor snapping at the soprano, who then snapped at the tenor. It took several hours of counselling to erase that from my memory. Something worse happened to a rather disliked conductor when I was in the prompt box. As an opening night surprise, someone whom he'd previously upset, presumably a member of the orchestra, removed the entire scene of 'In questa Reggia' from his full score. The terror on his face, because he'd never really learnt the score, was a picture.

There is a general type of soprano who sings the title role. It's unfortunate that they all seem to belong to the Clean Plate Club – women lacking in a waistline and delicate physical shape. The extra weight is not because one needs extra girth to sustain the vocal demands of the role. Perhaps it's the long hours by themselves in the hotel room with chocolates in the refrigerator? Throughout the last two decades some producers would pay for two first-class seats on the plane to accommodate their divas and rent limousines with extra space for travel comfort. I know of one entrepreneur who was called by a restaurant that advertised an 'all you can eat' breakfast begging him to stop his Turandot, who was staying in the apartment next door, from destroying his business. The same American soprano found it humorous when she got stuck in a revolving door and had to be pushed through by two hefty concierge attendants.

None of the Turandots with whom I've worked

have been members of the Clean Plate Club, but some of my colleagues have not been so lucky. Quite recently a soprano made her debut in London in the role. Her girth is such that she finds it hard to negotiate stairs so, instead of her climbing unaided to the top of the set for her first appearance, the company rented a hydraulic fork-lift. Unfortunately, all good intentions were destroyed when the weight of the soprano made it shudder. As the soprano emerged, the audience could clearly see her fleshy cheeks wobbling with every shudder of the unseen fork-lift. The same soprano speedily became known for her dramatic limitations when she insisted on performing the entire riddle scene seated on a stool. At first the stage crew thought she was 'just resting' during rehearsals but... The great Turandots of history – Rosa Raisa (the role's creator), Gina Cigna, Eva Turner, Maria Nemeth, Maria Jeritza, Birgit Nilsson, Ghena Dimitrova and Eva Marton – were not plump girls when they were in their Turandot heyday. Why is it the norm these days to have a larger than life Turandot?

Act Three starts with some moody music, swelling and subsiding for about three minutes. As it fades, the famous G major figure launches into what has been voted the most famous aria in the world, 'Nessun dorma' (No one shall sleep). Outside the opera house, it's sung by any and every male and female, usually without any idea of the aria's dramatic context. Popular vocalists sing it in whatever key is comfortable and in very approximate Italian. Please note that the word *stelle* with two l's means 'stars' and *stele* with one 'l' translates as 'obelisk'. There's a slight difference. If I never hear this aria, beyond an opera production, it will be too soon!

In short, Calaf – or the Unknown Prince – sings that Turandot is desperate to uncover his name and will not stop until she knows the answer. Rather than allow the tenor to enjoy the applause his high note evokes, Puccini sweeps us into a scene where Ping, Pang and (you guessed it) Pong try to extract the answer through temptation. They offer him sexual favours – not from them (that's only dressing room gossip) – but from scantily clad female dancers. They will even aid his escape from execution, not dissimilar to the story of Nanki Poo in Gilbert and Sullivan's *The Mikado*. Calaf rejects their kind offer and longs to be in the embrace of the Ice Princess Turandot.

She comes into view, along with PP&P and the entire chorus, dragging with her Timur and Liù. As she tortures Liù to extract the name, the slave girl sings an aria that is one of the most beautiful melodies in the score. No matter how much torture she endures, Liù will never give up the secret of the one she loves. This is quickly followed by a second, more dramatic aria, where Liù kills herself rather than see him love another. It's this kindness that wins her the heart of the audience. A good friend sang her first and only Liù with Franco Corelli as

Calaf and Brigit Nilsson as Turandot. There was no rehearsal and Corelli arrived at the theatre just in time to throw on some make-up and walk on stage, where he greeted her with a handshake and went on with the opera. His greeting must have been more than slightly puzzling for the audience. Even more curious was the undirected dropping of the suicide knife because illness had caused her hands to perspire and the dagger slipped and bounced on the stage – twice.

Liù dies, Timur weeps over her body and a funeral procession exits the stage. Unfortunately, at the school performance mentioned earlier, as Liù was being carried off following her suicide, one young charmer in the audience called in a very loud voice, 'Shag her while she's still warm!' That was a lovely memory that the soprano can pass on to her children. Calaf and Turandot are now alone together. This is where Franco Alfano took up his pen and wrote a fantastic duet, 'Principessa di Morte' (Princess of Death). Calaf is informed by Turandot that she is not mortal, but is the daughter of heaven, free and pure. After a couple of minutes, tenor embraces soprano and smacks a long kiss on her lips. The orchestra, resplendent with full brass, supports this moment of high emotion. As if a miracle has happened, Turandot's hard exterior melts away and she finds a tear on her cheek. Naturally she has to sing an aria about it. She realises her defeat and urges the Unknown Prince to leave with his secret. Secret? 'I give you my name and my life together as a gift. I am Calaf, son of Timur.'

Turandot finds a new energy, as does the orchestra. Offstage brass blares away. Electric currents emerge from the strings and the entire company moves back on stage. Turandot rejoices to her father: 'I know the stranger's name. His name is … love!' And guess what we hear? The chorus in full throttle singing of love, joy and laughter to the tune of 'Nessun dorma'. It's just what we all needed.

THE CHORUS

IT'S ONLY RIGHT and proper that I should begin by saluting the members of the chorus for their talent, commitment and patience. That said, I must add that the collective noun is a whinge of choristers.

A general audience member does not realise the importance of the chorus's work. Along with the music director, they are the staple of every opera company. The show cannot go on without them, unless you perform one of the small number of operas which do not include a chorus, and who'd want to see that? Being in the shadow of the stars can be a depressing thing and it is part of the chorister's plight to overcome this fact of life. In the past, producers used to encourage chorus singers to develop the skills to become principal artists. What's the difference between a soloist and a chorister? Being given the opportunity to shine and take command of the stage.

Some chorus members never come to terms with the fact that they are not playing the lead – 'My voice is as good as the diva's, if not better!' – but what they fail to understand is the 'it' factor. There is much more to being a star than merely possessing a voice of quality. As we all know, the best voices are in the chorus. Sometimes it's cruel that producers want those voices to remain there to make the sound more lustrous. Some principal singers started their careers in the chorus; a lot of them should have stayed there.

Opera choruses vary greatly from show to show. Rossini wrote only for men's chorus in his *The Barber of Seville* and *La Cenerentola*, while Puccini chose a baritone-free one for *Madama Butterfly*. These works require smaller numbers onstage than, say, the huge casts demanded by the score of *Lohengrin,* Modest Moussorgsky's *Boris Godounov* or Tchaikovsky's *Pique Dame*. Because choruses cut into the budget big time, producers tend to choose repertoire that asks for fewer choristers. Sometimes they go one step further. A 'modern' production of an opera by Handel might do without a chorus entirely. We still have the chorus music – but it's performed by the collected soloists/principals. This is tough on everyone. The chorus has an enormous workload. Principal artists sing about two or three times a week whereas a chorister might have four or five performances with rehearsals during the day for another two operas new to the repertoire.

Therefore choristers really like shows that enable them to go home early. The last thing they need is to be onstage, in costume and full make-up, at the final curtain – after all, there's a rehearsal for another opera early the next morning. This means that there'll be an extra 20 minutes before they're out of the building. If the costume is not too body hugging, a crafty chorister might conceal the fact that he or she is wearing their street attire underneath. I've seen this happen several times. Stranger still, I've been in the wings at the final curtain of a performance and experienced a chorister race offstage to avoid taking the bow, and hence get home earlier. When asked the reason, he responded with an honest, 'No one will notice one less body onstage.' A few days later, he was the one less body onstage. The producers managed to have him sacked.

If you need a reality check all you need to do is sit in the chorus dressing room for a few minutes. All those onstage and off are brought down to size. Whatever scandal has been connected with an artist in the past – or future – is added to the mixture. One of the greatest gifts a chorister has is that of impersonation. Some can mimic the principal artist better than the principal artist. I went through a stage, while a young rehearsal pianist, of giving cues in the voices of the singers with whom I was working. Some found it endearing; one must remember that the first thing one mimics is the fault in the instrument.

Chorus members sometimes have a lot of time on their hands during a performance, waiting for the next entry. Card games are favoured by the men, as are gossip sessions by the women. Although that sounds really sexist, it's true. A little distraction from the work on stage makes life more interesting.

Some of the text rewrites I've heard from choristers leave little to the imagination. They can be caustically correct, and on occasion depressingly honest. The striking thing is that they all rhyme. The male chorister can make the simplest, and most innocent, operatic phrase into something sordid. For example, when Ferrando sings the word 'Bugiarda' (meaning 'the liar') to the male chorus in the opening scene of *Il Trovatore*, they look at each other gleefully, nod their heads (a poor theatrical convention found in abundance in amateur productions) and silently mouth the name of that illustrious porn actor, 'Butch Harder'. I wait for this moment at each performance. And reality television thought they were the first to put a porn star on stage!

Onstage the chorus can create a whole sub-plot that would rival *The Bold and the Beautiful* or, quite easily, be more interesting. The slightest movement of a hand, a gesture or a glance can suggest a multitude of stories – all in addition to the director's concept. A chorister can make buying something as unimportant as a loaf of bread at a village market the biggest, and most important, gesture in that scene. Gone are the days when the chorus stood in straight lines or melted into the background.

I've rarely been accused of corrupting the chorus during a performance and it embarrasses me to relate this true tale. There was a time when I sat in the small box in the middle of the front of the stage prompting performances, a job that requires intense concentration. You prompt every singer with the first few words of their line as they take the breath to sing it. Timing is really important. As well as that, you cue the entries, pointing to the relevant singer so they know that it's their turn. It's very naughty to distract the performers from their performance. I was prompting an uncut reading of the Berlioz marathon, *Les Troyens*, which is about four hours longer than it should be. We had a bass in the ensemble who, on a good day, sounded like a car trying to start on a winter's morning. He was a nice man, if a little too serious, and the chorus found him incredibly boring as an artist and person. Eventually, I'd had enough too and, instead of cueing him visually with my finger, I made a gesture as though I was starting a car unsuccessfully. I still remember the twinkling eye of almost every member of the company as they continued to sing the endless score. Before that I was just a prompter. After this, I was one of them. Of course, that was years ago. Nowadays, I'm riddled with professionalism.

A performance of Wagner's very long opera *Die Meistersinger von Nürnberg* sees the chorus singing in the opening scene, joining in again for the fight scene at the conclusion of Act Two and then not appearing again until the final scene in Act Three. To save costs, producers sometimes engage an extra chorus to supplement the main chorus in the opening and closing scenes. The fight scene in the middle is so frantic anyway that you're actually not going to miss that extra body on stage. Those extra choristers have something like three and a half hours between their appearances. It's the only opera I know of where the participants are allowed to go out for a meal while the show is on.

Although the chorus has much to do in works like *Otello*, *La Traviata*, *Madama Butterfly*, *Tosca* and *La Bohème*, they complete their onstage job before the last act begins. For ticket-purchasing members of the audience it might be a disappointment to visualise the chorus standing in their day clothes, holding their bags, ready to leave the opera house while singing the offstage Humming Chorus, or *Tosca*'s offstage cantata, being the party revellers outside Violetta's window or singing the chorus in the inn in Act Three of *La Bohème*. As the last note ends, the choristers erase the onstage action from their minds and leave. That's art.

There are short straws to be picked too. The women are lucky in *Lucia di Lammermoor* – they leave a whole act before the men, who must wait to sing in the tomb scene. The same happens in *Madama Butterfly*, but there's less time to wait. After the Humming Chorus, which sees out Act Two, there are a few brief sailor calls. These days, most productions segue the second and third acts, so it's only a matter of five minutes more for the tenors to wait – there are no baritones or basses in the chorus of this opera.

A couple of pieces in the standard repertoire introduce the chorus much later. It isn't until the curtain of Act Two of *Die Fledermaus* that we see the stage filled with the guests at Orlofsky's party. The village folk arrive late-ish in Mozart's *The Marriage of Figaro,* as does the chorus in *The Magic Flute*. Because of the added cost of employing an actor or supernumerary, a director will ask a member of the chorus to perform a non-singing part in addition to his or her singing role. Tenors are particularly good at playing waiters; baritones are splendid as bouncers. Sopranos no longer in the flush of youth are excellent prostitutes in Act Three of *Manon Lescaut* and mezzos tend to play maids. Choristers can be the most creative of all opera creatures, perhaps because they have to show all their stagecraft in cameo roles. It's now or never and they perform with style – mostly. After all, if your entire part's 'Dinner is served' and you sing 'Sinner is derved' you've lost.

Here's a true story. A new chorister had kept his personal life quiet: he was an enigma to his colleagues. One morning there was no sign of him at a rather important rehearsal. The stage manager rang his home at regular intervals with no answer and they presumed that this was just another example of his nonchalant attitude. Several hours later he arrived at the rehearsal room and the stage manager was ready to go for the jugular. Before the onslaught could happen the chorister apologised profusely: 'I'm really sorry. My baby died!'

What could be said?

'Oh, how terrible. Are you okay? You should go home. Can we drive you? Is there anything we can do to help?'

'No. I'll be all right. Let me join the rehearsal.'

It wasn't until about a year later that it was discovered that he never had a baby, a wife or even anybody who actually liked him.

Another time, to win sympathy when arriving late for a rehearsal, he said that he'd just received news that he only had a year to live. Time passed and he bounced into the dressing room to discover his place covered with gifts of flowers and chocolates. A fellow chorister explained: 'Exactly a year ago, you told us, in detail, that you were mortally ill and had only 12 months to live. Well, it's exactly 12 months to the day and we want your last day on earth to be memorable!'

ENCORE

THERE'S A RATHER schmaltzy, but melodious, operetta by the Hungarian composer Emmerich Kalman which contains a song translated as 'Where are they now?' One may well ask the same about opera singers.

Those fabulous singing celebrities who come complete with glorious voice, unique artistry (note that I didn't write 'great') and enormous egos are dropping off the planet quicker than Cecilia Bartoli can sing coloratura. First Franco Corelli was called to audition for his big agent in the sky, a week later Franco Bonisolli hung up his boxing gloves, then Renata Tebaldi and Victoria de los Angeles left us. Birgit Nilsson and Elisabeth Schwarzkopf went to higher ground, and the divine Anna Moffo was gathered before her time. A few days apart Régine Crespin and Beverly Sills departed their myriad of fans and, a month later, Lucky Luciano found that he wouldn't be feasting on any more pasta. So many

279

great and much admired voices have recently been silenced.

Let me share with you a story that would seem impossible today.

In the late 1950s a mammoth production of Umberto Giordano's blockbuster opera *Andrea Chénier* was set to open a newly built auditorium in Los Angeles. Sharing top billing were two great Italian-born vocal deities, Renata Tebaldi and Franco Corelli. At the time there were no better celebrities to hear in these particular roles. Giordano's 'stand and deliver' – or 'park and bark' – opera can only work well if you have big personalities with big voices on stage and Tebaldi and Corelli were the epitome of this grand delivery style.

Opening night came and the invited audience read like a list of the rich and famous.

Tebaldi and Corelli arrived in separate limousines an hour before curtain and emerged looking like the stars they were. Tebaldi, wrapped in a fabulous fur coat was dressed to the nines for the high-profile supper after the performance. As usual, both stars were clutching their favourite pet poodles. A falafel-brained security guard stopped them as they were about to pass through the stage door and instructed them that a bill had been passed forbidding animals to be in public buildings. Without questioning the guard, Tebaldi and Corelli, complete with pooches, made a 180-degree turn and went back to their waiting limousines, to the amazement of the gathering crowd. Several minutes went by and the general manager appeared, asking the whereabouts of the night's stars. When the security guard muttered that they'd been turned away because they refused to enter without the comfort of their pets he was immediately made redundant and a hasty call to the city mayor modified the legislation to allow pets in public buildings for the next 24 hours. The limousine doors opened and Tebaldi, Corelli and dogs filed through the stage door and sang their hearts out through a very loud performance of *Andrea Chénier*.

These days opera is presented to audiences in many different guises. We have all been exposed to the phenomenon of the Three Tenors, the arena/event opera concerts and the 'vogue' opera groups. Since that famous 1990 concert that initially united Placido Domingo, José Carreras and Luciano Pavarotti on stage, the opera world has changed enormously. For fear of losing more face than I already have, I won't give my personal opinion on the notion of what is presently accepted as an opera singer. Suffice to say that it is difficult to reconcile cross-over artists, winners of popular television shows and slickly dressed, cleverly marketed singing groups with anything that resembles classical singing. If you glance through the shelves in most record stores you will be presented with discs of opera singers who have never appeared in an opera. At least the Three

Tenors had substantial operatic careers behind them when they sang 'Nessun dorma' as a trio. Is it something of a paradox that while price structures within opera houses increase opera's élitism and make it less accessible to the masses, phenomena like the Three Tenors and Opera in the Park actually take it to a wider audience? Producers must be clicking their heels in glee.

It's up to us to make this new era of opera the next golden age. We must seek out the glories as well as the quirks in our operatic culture. I constantly hear the oldies remembering the good old days as if those standards were now unattainable. It is my intention to encourage the current generation of opera singers to build on the knowledge of the past and learn from those great voices and unique personalities. For now we have the stories and I hope there are a lot more to come.

Next time you're in town, drop in to my place for a cup of hot chocolate and I'll give you an update.